The Way of the Dog

The Way of the Dog

GEOFF BURCH

CAPSTONE

The right of Geoff Burch to be identified as the author of this book has been asserted in accordance with the Copyright, Designs and Patents Act 1988

First published 2005 by
Capstone Publishing Limited (a Wiley Company)
The Atrium
Southern Gate
Chichester
West Sussex
PO19 8SQ
www.wileyeurope.com
E-mail (for orders and customer service enquiries): cs-books@wiley.co.uk

CIP catalogue records for this book are available from the British Library and the US Library of Congress

ISBN 1-84112-576-8

Typeset in Adobe Caslon Pro by Sparks, Oxford
(www.sparks.co.uk)

Printed and bound in Great Britain by TJ International Ltd, Padstow, Cornwall

This book is printed on acid-free paper responsibly manufactured from sustainable forestry in which at least two trees are planted for each one used for paper production

Dedication

To my wonderful wife, friend, boss, and owner, Sallie, who as everybody knows is the real brains behind the whole thing.

To my sons, James and Simon, whose successes have exceeded anything that I could have ever achieved and who have soared like eagles from our cuckoo's nest.

Contents

Acknowledgements   ix

The Way of the Dog —
The Story about the Story   xi

The Way of the Dog —
Instructions for Use   xliii

The Way of the Dog   1

The Way of the Dog
in a Nutshell   123

About the Author   127

Acknowledgements

- My commissioning editor, John Moseley, for all his help and support.
- My friend, Paul Hurst, whose intensive scrutiny has corrected the errors of my ways (well, my pen, anyway).
- All my clients, whose adventures have been the inspiration to the story.

The Way of the Dog

The Story about the Story

Success, who needs it?

I am often accused – falsely, I hope – of being a motivational speaker, so inevitably on my travels to various conferences I bump into the genuine article. They get their audiences breaking bits of wood, pushing arrows to their throats, and even walking through fire. I watch aghast and can never see the point. What is it that people are getting? What do they gain from the dubious ability to walk through fire? Even more frightening is that, after one of my own tirades, people will come up to me and say they feel motivated and even inspired. Inspired to what? I wrote this book to try and help people get what they want, but what do they want? One conclusion I draw from this is that whatever it is that they *do* want, they don't want what they've got now, and the classic motivator can take them somewhere else at least. When I discuss this the professionals ramble on about visualization and goal setting, but these are very difficult if all you know is 'anything is better than this'.

Apparently, what you should do is choose your ideal situation and visualize it. In a more businesslike or career situation, you should set goals, targets, or objectives. However, this has never motivated me; it is more likely to confuse me and leave me feeling that I have failed at something. Exactly what I have failed at, I don't have the foggiest idea.

It surprised me then when people said that I was successful. Successful at what? Successful, I suppose, at the things I set out to do. Therefore, bearing in mind my hearty and deep-felt cynicism, how could this be? Can ordinary, well-adjusted, fed-up people achieve whatever they want without some loopy Pollyanna view of the world? Could it be a simple process that, if deconstructed, could be bottled and

sold with a guarantee? Perhaps, instead of goals and so on, we see what we want as a destination to journey towards.

An atlas of optimism

To make the journey logical, we need a starting point so that we can measure from where we are to where we need to be. Sometimes, we might find the distance too great to make the thing worth bothering with. If a journey is made from one place to another, the usual starting place is where you are at the moment. The first problem, therefore, is to have a very clear idea of where you are in the scheme of things. I love the joke of the person asking the way and being told, 'If I wanted to get there, I wouldn't start from here!' Well, you do start from here, so be certain where *here* is and don't fool yourself into thinking you are somewhere else.

Actually, here's a profound (stupid, but still profound and faintly encouraging nonetheless) thought about journeys. You start off from where you are and travel toward your destination. After some time travelling, you stop for a rest and to take stock. Where you have stopped is a place too – in fact it is where you are now. When you measure that against your destination, it stands to reason that your original journey should be shorter – in other words, you are getting closer to where you want to be. If your destination is further or the same as it always was, you have cocked something up. If you drive on the highway and you see your destination is 50 miles away on a signpost, and at the next post it says 40 miles, things are going well. If it says 60 miles, you are going in the opposite direction. If, after a few hours of travelling, it still says 50 miles, you are going sideways. It makes sense, then, to see a signpost as quickly into your journey as possible. It would also be good to have a trustworthy road atlas or map.

Imagine having a positive-thinking or self-help atlas that when you look at the distance from London to Glasgow says, 'It's not as far as you think!'.

And how to get there? The positive-thinking atlas says, 'Imagine that you are there, picture yourself standing in Glasgow. Believe you can do it and one day you will wake up and find yourself there'. Complete rubbish, of course. A real road atlas shows the routes, the distances, and the places along the way. Actually, if I was being difficult, I might think about charts (as in sailing boats and ships, etc.): in a boat – particularly a sailing boat – you can make

progress towards your destination without necessarily going straight there. You use your chart to find hidden dangers and surging tides. If the wind is against you, then you must tack. If your destination is 50 miles away, you might sail for 25 miles and find your destination is now 40 miles away. This won't discourage a sailor because they know that they are making progress, and they happily tack away.

An important point here is that one of the keys of safety at sea is knowing exactly where you are at all times.

Fear is the key

The first time I saw all this stuff work in my life was when I was young and first married, and we had clocked up a bank overdraft that threatened to sink us without trace. The day this monster hit the limit was a huge shock. We had been drifting along day to day and, of course, at the back of my mind I sort of understood that we were spending more than we were earning – but what the heck, something would turn up. Something turned up alright, in the shape of a very nasty letter from the bank manager which, in effect, said enough was enough and could they have their money back or else. I scampered round the house like a headless chicken. This was it, I had hit the wall and there was nowhere to go.

What I didn't realize was that this was the perfect place to start a journey, because the bank had told me exactly where I was – up to my neck in it. The essence of a good journey is to understand clearly your current position, and I had certainly done that. Next, a destination is required. I had that too, I had to be in the black. I announced that we would have a slap-up feast when the overdraft was cleared, but until then nothing was more important.

I would hate people to think I was obsessive but, like everyone, under the right circumstances I can be a bit of a picture-straightener. Who hasn't lain in bed thinking, 'Did I leave the hot plate on?' You know you didn't. You checked didn't you? So turn over, and go to sleep. Forget it. Forget it warming up that hanging tea towel – which is just starting to smoulder – a flicker of flame, the safety film that told you a blazing kitchen could reach a temperature of a blast furnace in only 25 seconds after the first glowing ember. Darn it! Off you pad, downstairs, to find that of course you turned it off. If you can develop a destination that creates the sort of itch that can't be scratched, then it all starts to happen. I started to chase down money

that was owed to me (why should I be hammered by my bank, when people owed *me* money); I looked at jobs that had the wrong mathematics, i.e. cost £10, revenue £9 – a bit of smart adjustment soon changed that to cost £10, revenue £11. I also became a bit of a pain in the neck with the 'can we afford it' routine. The signposts were easy: every few days I checked the account and, as long as the big red figure grew smaller, we were reaching that destination. If it ever grew bigger, then swift action was taken to put it back on track. Inevitably, the day came when the first black bank statement arrived, and we went to the restaurant 'Del Posh' and had our feed.

Sounds simple, but I hadn't realized what I had done. I had been driven by fear and shock and, although there was some sense of achievement, there was no fun in it.

Destinationless obsessions can be even dodgier. People who write books like this should keep things light, and should probably keep away from areas that bring tragedy to other people's lives. After all, this should be a nice, cheery, easy book that at best will bring you nothing but good fortune. But, I must get this one thought off my chest, and it concerns anorexia. (Please accept, though, that this is just my thought and in no way do I want to diminish the gravity of this awful affliction.) This nasty beast has all the trademarks of a journey. It starts from a known position (a weight), control is taken, and clear signposts are there – a pound here and a kilo there – taking it on and on, driven, controlled, but with no destination. The journey is the obsession, not the destination. If there is nowhere to stop, then it doesn't stop. When my wife used to worry about the tight ship I was running, I could say, 'I can't stop, I haven't got there yet, we must clear that overdraft'. But what happens if that is simply 'I can't stop'? They can never get there because there was simply nowhere to get to in the first place.

Perhaps it is a little less worrying, but people can become 'wealth-orexics'. I have a friend who has built up a building and property business from nothing. He has an investment and property portfolio worth millions, all steadily grown with care and hard work. He has grown children with good jobs but, because of their parsimonious upbringing, they are itching to get their hands on his money – which does them no good at all. He still drives the same old van he had from the beginning, and they still live in the same small house in a very unfashionable part of town. I pointed out to him that, now he is middle-aged, if he stopped and sold up – cashed in his chips – however

hard he tried, he wouldn't live long enough to spend it all, so what was the point of the accumulation of wealth with no destination?

So easy, a kid could do it

All these thoughts have formed the genesis of this book: a simple, controllable recipe for success. So, why produce what appears to be a kids' story? Bizarrely enough, while this appears to be by way of an introduction, I have already written the main story, which I have re-read and had a good think about. When writers write, why do they do it and what goes through their mind? Is my destination a best-seller, or will I be delighted just to amuse and entertain you? So, as I read the body of this book and feel that maybe it might be a bit obvious, perhaps, if it can assure the success that you want for yourself, it's OK to go the easy way.

A dog's life

I had success with a book called *Resistance is Useless*, which I suppose was mostly a book on sales. But, among the stories, tales, and examples in the book, my personal favourite was the allegory of the sheepdog. I had watched a dog herding sheep and, at the time, it was the perfect example of a classic sale. The dog would take the herd of sometimes reluctant and difficult sheep from one place to another: from where the sheep were, to a clear destination – usually a pen or enclosure. Along the way, the dog would encounter obstacles such as prickly hedges, streams, and trees. The thing that got me going was that the dog never ever failed. Sure sometimes a bad sheep would break loose and have to be rounded up, or the whole herd would refuse at an obstacle, but whatever happened the dog would get the sheep to the pen. In sheepdog competitions the judging is done against the clock. The question is never 'Will the dog succeed?' but 'When will the dog succeed?' I know that, with a little anthropomorphism, we like to think 'clever dog' or even 'cleverer-than-me dog', but animal psychologists will tell you that this is impossible. The dog probably doesn't even have the ability to have an abstract thought. One eminent man made the statement that dogs have two states of being: they are either happy, or waiting to be happy. The lack of abstract thought prevents them from having a future to be frightened of, they don't feel despair or fatigue with repetition. When the shepherd sends them after

the flock, they don't return saying, 'Oh, wow! Those sheep are miles away, and there are so many obstacles. It makes me so depressed – haven't you got any easier sheep? Anyway, I herded loads of sheep yesterday. Can't I do some tractor driving?'

The reality is that the shepherd sends the dog off, and the first thing the dog does is to establish clearly where the sheep are in the great pattern of things. It doesn't worry or upset the dog – these feelings are alien to it. The sheep are where the sheep are, and the dog gets them moving towards their destination until it encounters an obstacle. Unlike a human, who is bitterly aware of the many more obstacles to come and may be tempted to give up there and then, the dog sees just this one obstacle. Its memory of the last obstacle gave it experience – not bad feelings – and it cares nothing for the difficulty or gravity of any forthcoming ones. It deals with them one at a time until the sheep are safely penned, and then it bounds back ready for the next lot. If there are no more sheep to herd, it puts all thoughts of sheep out of its head and lives a life of pleasurable doggy things like eating, lying in front of the fire nibbling its bottom, or parenting and loving its pups.

For *Resistance is Useless*, it was the lit motive for the perfect sale. If the sheep were customers, they are where they are, which is probably not currently doing business with us. When we try to herd them to our pen, we encounter obstacles: 'We don't know you well enough to do business with us'; 'We are happy with the people we've got'; 'We won't pay these prices'. Of course, the dog wouldn't do all the work of managing those obstacles only to reach the gate of the pen and then give up. Picture the scene, the dog runs up to the shepherd, tail wagging, tongue lolling, a happy dog. The shepherd asks, 'Well, how did you get on with the sheep?'.

'Great!'

'No obstacles?'

'Yep, but I dealt with each and every one of them.'

'Sheep in the pen?'

'Well no, but they are very interested in it!'

It just doesn't happen.

It just isn't natural

I was delighted by the success of *Resistance is Useless* and so was my publisher. Other books followed and, thankfully, were also well received.

'Do us another one, Geoff,' shrieked the publishers, capering and hopping around like demented goblins. Now, if publishers are desperate for the next book, the author should be able to push his luck just a little. My *bête noire* has always been titles: *Resistance* was written as 'Piddling on the Yucca Plants'; *Go It Alone* had something to do with guerrillas; and *Writing on the Wall* had the innocuous title 'Arming the Peasants' – banned because apparently, in my American market, it might encourage rebellion! So this time I could choose, couldn't I? I had received a lot of comments about the sheepdog thing. Could I expand on it? Could the dog thing be a sales process on its own? Could it be broken into simple, memorable steps? Could I produce a book around just this one idea? Yep. And 'Doing it Doggy Style' was born – result, uproar! I was instantly carpeted.

The chief troll rose from his chair and grasped the front edge of his desk as he pushed his twisted features toward me. I detected the smell of partially digested children on his fetid breath.

'Doggy Style?' he howled, 'Doggy Style – you know what that's about, don't you?'

'No,' I replied innocently, 'The book's about a business style that mimics the tenacity of a dog, that's all.'

'That's not all!' he cried, his voice shaking with emotion, large moon-like eyes shimmering from the gloom around him. Creaking, crackling voices grated their muted approval. He reached a frothing crescendo and, with a pointing skeletal finger, cried, 'It's a perversion!'.

'A perversion, yes, a perversion,' the voices echoed.

'How would you know?' I asked.

'We know because ...,' there was a tense silence.

'Our money, you change it.'

A simple sale simply makes money ...

So, here we are with *The Way of the Dog*, but serendipitously (is there such a word?), the change in title has broadened my thinking from creating a simple sales book, to a high-level sales book, to a management book, to a lifestyle book that can deal with personal success. But let's not gallop too far ahead. First, that simple sale.

The word 'sales' usually makes most civilians shrivel with horror. 'High Pressure' they cry, but what is high pressure? Making people buy things

that they don't want or need? Maybe not taking 'No' for an answer? Of course people don't want to buy from you. They don't want to pay the price that gives you a modest profit; they don't want to change from their current supplier. A sale is always about getting people to do what they don't want to do. That spotty youth wants your Ferrari, he wants the women flocking to him, and he loves the surging power and the admiring glances of his mates. You don't have to sell him those things, he has already bought them. What he doesn't want to do is to pay, to spend his hard-earned cash. That is the sales skill, getting him to do what he doesn't want to do – hand over the cash. If you have just started a business and are waiting for the customers to drift in and give you money, surprisingly they will. Just as in a field with sheep and a pen in it, some sheep will drift into that pen. It is just that the sheepdog can put all the sheep in the pen and keep them there whenever it wants to. In business we worked out a rough ratio of unherded customers, and came to the conclusion that four-fifths of potential business is lost this way – a 500 per cent rise in business GONE. At conferences for small and start-up business, I tell them these stories and tell them to develop the intention to sell. The idea of per centages like that tends to light their fire and I inevitably get someone becoming a pain in the neck by trying to flog me something. They will not take no for an answer, but does the dog take no for an answer?

'Come on sheep!'

'Baah, no thanks.'

'Oh OK, I'll leave it then.'

But, as we will see in the story, what happens when the dog rushes at the sheep barking? Of course they scatter, just like I do, frightened off by aggression. So we tend to adopt the opposite tack which is just as stupid.

'Oh, hi sheep, really nice of you to see me.'

'Baaaah.'

'I can see you are busy grazing, so I won't keep you. Can I just point out that there is a pen at the bottom of the field, if you would like to be shut in it I'll leave you with a brochure and my card. Bleat if you need anything.'

The idiot then writes in a report, 'Saw sheep, they were very interested'. Actually, with experience, they develop a shorthand and write, 'V.INT'. The sheep are left bewildered – 'Baah, who was that?'

The story shows the perfect controlled herd from position to destination: the completely controlled profitable sale in an easy-to-master package.

... But a major sale makes more money

But the major sale, could that be so easy? In *Resistance is Useless* I took some time to define the difference between a normal and a major sale, but a little reprise shouldn't do any harm and certainly the connection with sheep, dogs and pens should be clarified. Before we get into that, some new developments that have crept into business should be examined.

The traditional industrial buyer was seen as a monster, famously tough and even insulting. In one of the first books on sales I ever read, a buyer had pictures of sailing yachts on his wall. When an un-suspecting sales rep made a jolly comment like, 'Oh, boats, do you like sailing?' this creature then replied, 'I hate sailing. Those pictures are there to remind me that so much time gets wasted, so get down to busi-ness'. This was supposed to intimidate the seller and soften things up for a great deal, but then the big and intelligent companies started to have a re-think.

Say a major aero engine company had a sta-tionery buyer, in the old days he would have four hundred paper-clip suppliers on his list. Playing one off against the other, he could achieve an extra point one or even point two per cent discount. The companies examined this process, discovered it was costing them thousands in cash and hours of time. When all was said and done, a paper clip was a paper clip; its value was in its facile ability to hold bits of paper together. It certainly wasn't process critical (in other words, they didn't use paper clips as a key component in their engines, or at least I hope they didn't). What they had to do was to fire the idiot from Buying, saving thousands, cut the suppliers' list from four hundred to five or so, specify the perfect clip, find a supplier who could be trusted on cost and quality, and tell them to fire their representative – thus knocking his salary off the bottom line. To look at it a different way, you don't want people deep in your organization who know all there is to know about paper clips discussing the finer points with someone who is equally expert from the supplier's side. The simple value is in the simple product. These people, however clever, can add no value to your organization whatsoever – they just add cost.

This simple idea has been grasped with both hands and could probably represent a whole new book, if I ever get round to writing it. For us sellers, it can present a problem because, if we are canvassing for business, a great deal of our potential targets no longer have to shop around buyers, but are developing long-term partnerships with their suppliers. This means new customers are much harder to find, and are worth hanging on to when we do find them.

The internet helps us do nothing on a bigger scale

I tell a story about using the correct level of pressure to my audiences. It works – if it works at all – on a few levels; one of these is the customer care chestnut but that's another story; for now, let's think about the intention to sell. If you have a business, you need customers. I suppose on a motivational level, if you have a life, you need to make things happen. Making things happen frightens all of us to death. If we have a product or a service, we may put in an advert or send leaflets, and then we wait for things to happen which they don't. Now we have the internet we can have a rib-tickling website designed, and things can fail to happen on a global level – people all over the world can see our offering and not do business with us. At the risk of appearing totally sad, I remember a song called *Living Next Door to Alice*, about a guy who, from childhood, fell in love with his next-door neighbour Alice. For years and years he loved her but said nothing, until she married someone else and moved away. I actually shout, caper, and shake my fists in fury and frustration at the radio when that one comes on. The song was a huge hit because it strikes a chord; we sometimes know what we want, but we don't often have the bottle to ask for it.

People come up to me and say, 'For an idiot you are surprisingly successful. What is your secret, is it something you read?' Well yes, it was something I read. It was a t-shirt I had when I was a hippy. On the front of it there were two vultures sitting on a branch and one vulture is saying to the other vulture, 'Patience my arse, I'm going to go and kill something!' Making it happen can be scary (unless you are a sheepdog, and then it is just a job to be done), but scary can become fun. Fear, instead of crushing, excites. In the end, selling becomes like sport – the harder the challenge the more fun! If you enjoy golf, of course you would love a game with Tiger Woods, and of course you will get a whipping, but what fun! How your game will have improved! I did the same when looking for potential customers, the tougher the better. This one guy had refused to give me an appointment. For six years he had resisted my every effort, so I started sending him anniversary cards: 'Congratulations, you have resisted me for another year'.

Eventually he cracked, just a bit, but enough.

'Look, you are driving me mad. OK, if it will get you off my back, I will give you a five minute appointment. But let me warn you, we have been doing business with the same people for 25 years, we are delighted with their products, we are delighted with their service, and it's owned and run by my brother!'

I better finish the story now for the sake of continuity, but when I have finished we will go back and deal with a whinge and a possible solution.

The story unfolds with me visiting, weaving my magic spell and signing them up. Six years of my life invested, but it was worth it. The biggest contract we had ever had.

The next day our driver arrived to deliver whatever it was that we had been selling, and the woman at reception said, 'Oh, are you the new driver?'.

'Yep.'

'Could you carry the boxes upstairs, please?'

'Nope.'

'The other driver used to.'

'Well I'm not the other driver. You carry them yourself, you lazy cow.'

Some ten seconds later, they had cancelled. Six years of my life gone in ten seconds. I went mad. I found this driver and spent an hour kicking him round the car park but, to my horror, my boss found me and said, 'Hmm, Geoff, bit embarrassing this, but apparently you have assaulted one of the drivers'.

'Too right' I replied.

'Well, Geoff, look,' he explained, 'Salesman are very easy to find, but good drivers are not'.

Let's take the stories point by point from the top, and also find out that whinge.

Choose your target

Firstly, what I was doing was indulging in 'targeted selling'. You are capable of doing business with a number of people that you are not currently doing business with. What you do is to target those potential customers.

Example: you are an accountant. The Ford Motor Company uses someone else as their accountant, therefore you are not the Ford Motor Company's accountant. You decide you will become the Ford Motor Company's accountant (this is probably going to become a major sale). Ford is in a certain position as regards accountancy and they need to be moved to a position where they do business with you. A simple visit will give you an idea of their position, and the

obstacles that remain between here and there. By removing each obstacle, the Ford account is yours. Think and work like that sheepdog and the world's your lobster – easy-peasy. This is where the whinge starts. My wife – who is my manager, boss, chum, and owner – was listening to these cheery ideas for this section.

'Well, that's depressing,' she smiled in a dangerously mirthless way. 'I thought this book was the ultimate guide to making success inevitable?'

'Yep,' I rejoined, trying to bring in a note of cheerfulness.

'Well, if I made paper clips, I would be pretty upset. You've more or less said that I've got *no* chance of getting business from the mega-global jet engine corporation, now that they have sacked their buyer, got a long term stationery relationship, and couldn't give a toss about talking to anyone else.'

'Well I suppose you might have a point,' I conceded humbly. She wasn't placated.

'So, halfwit,' (term of endearment, I'm sure), 'What's the solution?'

I take her point. For this book to be helpful, we need to understand the changes that the world of business has gone through.

A popular disaster is to rely on the idea of a decision maker. The old sales books, possibly quite rightly, used to maintain that there was this mythical figure: the 'Decision Maker'. If we go back to the stationery buyer and the paper clips, he was your man, but the myth has been perpetuated long beyond its sell-by date. There is often no decision maker as such, but this must still be the subject of a lot of sales training. Take my own example. Geoff Burch Management Ltd is a fairly modest-sized company and we all do our bit but, because of the complications of modern life, we have to concentrate on the job in hand, i.e. speaking at conferences, producing books, and developing consultancy and training. Therefore, when a well-trained canvasser from a major telecom company telephones and says, 'Who is in charge of purchasing your telecommunications solutions?' everyone is a bit aghast. I think this happens a lot, and a new approach is needed.

How big?

I suppose it might be a good idea here to define a so-called major sale. It might be said that a small sale

involves one buyer, one decision, one price, in one moment: for instance, the purchase of a light bulb.

I sit, pensive and moody, studying my yellow documents by the light of a flickering light bulb. (Flickering?) 'Plink!' I am plunged into darkness and I set off forthwith to my corner shop to buy a bulb. Need is established, cost within certain boundaries is the only concern.

'How much are your 60-watt light bulbs?'

'Fifty quid'

'No thanks.'

I try elsewhere: sale failed.

'How much are your 60-watt light bulbs?'

'One pound.'

'Lovely, I'll have one.'

Sales success.

In major sales, how do you measure success? You have made an appointment with the chief executive of Mega Corporation to discuss his company using your state-of-the-art computer system, at a modest cost of 46 million pounds. He likes you, thinks the system is neat, so you try for a cheque for 46 million. 'Call it 45 for cash.' When he stops laughing, he explains that this may all take some time.

So, did you succeed or fail in this major sale? If you are a traditionalist, you will reply, 'I think it went very well'.

The problem is that you are just travelling hopefully. You are not in control of the process and, if you use our journey analogy, you don't have the foggiest idea where you are. Of course, our sheepdog always knows where it is. It knows where it started (position), it knows where it is going, and at any moment it knows its current position in relation to start and finish. If you asked it how it was doing, it wouldn't say, 'V. interested', 'Looking good', 'I'm very optimistic'. It would say 'I am 147.63 metres and 23 minutes from the pen'. Less emotional, but a lot more useful.

Fixing the machine

At the bottom of the sales heap lies the much-derided door-to-door salesperson. Their simple view of life is a numbers game. Knock on each and every door, repeat the same speech, and a certain per centage will buy. If five out of every hundred buy, and you want to double your sales, then call on two hundred people. Small changes to the speech make small improvements to the sales. The high flyers mock this and

claim to apply science to the major sale, using ideas like 'solution selling', 'relationship selling' and so on, but, at the end of it all, their key measure is conversion rate. In other words, the numbers game with a posher name; they measure outcomes. Suppose you had a machine that made cakes, an inscrutable black box into which you put ingredients and, at the other end, some cakes popped out. But only 10 per cent of these cakes are perfect and all nicely iced with a cherry in the middle; the rest are inedible wreckage. You could not, and would not, tolerate that; sales managers do. Truthfully, if 90 per cent of the cakes were perfect and only 10 per cent wreckage, you still wouldn't tolerate it; a sales manager would be dancing with hysterical happiness.

Firstly, you would not be happy with an inscrutable machine and would soon have the cover off to see how it made cakes. There is no point in making the whole machine fast or slow, or giving it more or less power. It is the bits of the machine that would interest you: 'Look, the cherry lifting arm squashes half the cherries. The egg breaker leaves bits of shell in every fourth cake.'

You will see that things go wrong at the very beginning and then the machine wastes its time processing an already knackered cake.

If you target potential customers in your profile of a typical customer, you should be able to sell to all of them. If not, you should be able to see where failure occurs and put this right, so that the next time you do sell to everyone you approach. I once had a lynch mob after me for suggesting that sales, service, design, marketing, and production should all sit down together to create the perfect customer product. Picture the scene:

'I could have sold them in red.'

'We could design them in red.'

'We can build them in red, but they will cost more.'

'Price wasn't the issue.'

It sounds so simple that it doesn't even need saying, but the above very rarely happens. It is more, 'We build them and you flog 'em'.

The mole hunt

Just to stop for a moment, I learned the fallacy of the 'one decision maker' thing a long time ago, and gained a huge advantage over my competitor by developing a minimum of FOUR decision makers.

First, I saw the chief executive of Mega Corporation. He loves my cake maker but he can't sign today. Most people wait here for the decision, but who has to use this machine?

Second, we see Sid Bloggs in production. This marvellous machine could double his output, but in his mind he is thinking, does it make him work twice as hard, or cut his paid hours?

'How's the new machine, Sid?' asks El Supremo.

'Just can't get on with it, your mightiness. It is certainly lower quality.'

We are dead in the water. Let's see Sid before the demonstrator is put in, and show how it makes his life easier, safer, and more secure.

Ok, they're happy, but who's paying for it? The finance director is worried: capital expenditure was not part of his plan. Show him how it saves money, how it pays back within 12 months, and how you could tailor the lease to vanish from his books.

Finally, I would hang around the local bars to develop an insider or mole – a forklift driver or receptionist who can give me the gossip.

'You know that weird kid with big ears who works in purchasing, that's the CEO's son!'

'The finance director has had a big row with Acme Cake-O-Matic about their invoicing.'

Think of the herd, not the single sheep.

To sum up, by taking the machine to bits, by knowing where we are at all times, we can make success inevitable.

A dog is for life, not just for business

That is how a sheepdog works: simple, controlled persistence, a clear view of what has been done, and what is needed. The dog knows exactly where it is and when it encounters an obstacle it deals with that obstacle only, not stressing about past or future ones.

As I prepared this book to be a predominantly business book, it occurred to me that people with nothing to sell would like their lives to go in a certain direction. They would like to achieve goals, fame, wealth, the perfect cheese soufflé, and all the same rules apply. Most of us have no idea where we are. We may know where we would like to be, but have no idea how far away it is, or what would be the first step to take, or what to do if we encounter obstacles. Success is something we all wish for, but we find it hard to believe that it could be inevitable.

This book has been surprisingly difficult to write and my poor old publisher has been tearing his hair to get hold of the manuscript, so when the body of the book appeared to be a kids' story, they went bonkers. The justification for this is that, it is said, to start to be fluent in a foreign language you should try reading children's books, and, to us, success is a foreign land. I wanted to create a recipe book of success for you that can be absorbed at airports, on journeys, or in a few minutes of spare time. And, of course, it will be one of the few commercial books that you could read to the kids. You never know, they could find success before you do!

Good luck, and on with the story.

The Way of the Dog

Instructions for Use

First of all, enjoy the story! *The Way of the Dog* is full of hidden messages and lessons, some of them so well hidden that, now I have written it, I can't find them again myself. A few have been pulled out and, if you like, you can read them as you go. Personally, I find footnotes and so on a distraction. I prefer to finish the tale and then go back for the notes – but it is up to you. The most important thing is to let the book provoke you into thinking about your own situation. Get your own messages from it, and let them guide you to the success you want for yourself. If you do find more good things, let me know – I would love to hear your interpretation.

The Way of the Dog

GEOFF BURCH

AS HE TRUDGED THROUGH THE RAIN with his case of samples, Derek Stubbins knew that he wasn't a failure. He was a success that people had failed to acknowledge; he was a success that events had conspired to thwart; he was a millionaire in waiting; he just hadn't had the lucky breaks that a lot of his colleagues had received. Hadn't he run his own hugely successful hand-made chocolate business, until it had gone bust before anyone had given it a chance? That wasn't his fault either, it was the recession. Of course, other similar enterprises had succeeded but they had insider information that Derek had never been privy

to. He would make such a great millionaire as well
– he felt that he was born to it. His natural talent
was the management and spending of a large fortune.
Being stuck with the paltry money that he currently
earned was what caused the difficulties. If someone
could just wave a magic wand and make him fabu-
lously rich, he could show his real worth – his ability
to be a magnanimous gentleman, lavishing luxury on
the poor! He could demonstrate his forgiving nature
by even helping his enemies, and all those who put
him down and failed to acknowledge his true gifts.

The cold puddles ebbed and flowed from the hole
in his shoe, and he gave a grim smile as he thought of
the famous Irishman giving directions, 'If I was you,
I wouldn't start from here!' Exactly, he shouldn't start
from here. No man could start from here. A wife who
was in despair at the state of their home and finances,
kids who treated him with contempt, friends who
not only failed to accept his status but who obviously
whispered to each other that he was a prat, and now
this awful job selling double glazing. OK, he was a
great salesman, it was just that customers failed to
respond positively. They were so slow, so thick, so
tiresome. Maybe his impatience with them showed a
little bit, but he felt that he hid it well. The truth was
that he should be in management, it was here that his

abilities lay, if only his short-sighted bosses could see it. He was too talented and intelligent to be in the front line. Of course, when you had an IQ the size of his, you would become bored with the mundane chore of order taking. With a team to lead and inspire, things would be different – the challenge of leading by example, bringing on the less able, group meetings where they would hang on his every word. As it was, he was on final warning to be fired. FIRED! That's a good one – fired from a scabby, commission-only job that no one wanted to do. Just because it had been a while since he had sold anything. That wasn't his fault either. His enemies at the office had clearly lumbered him with the worst territory. He was tempted to chuck his sample case over the nearest hedge and go home, but telling the family that yet another hope had died was probably straying into last-straw territory.

On and on he walked, through an estate of modest houses; there was no point in calling on them, they wouldn't have the money. Then there was a road of huge detached houses, even less point with them; they set the dogs on itinerant salespeople. On and on he walked, stumping, sighing, and feeling down; on and on until he had left the town completely. He wandered through miles of countryside without a house in sight. Part of him felt anxious about the lack of potential customers, and the bigger part felt relieved that he would not have to confront any more belligerent strangers. The road led into a large, dark forest, which meant more walking and even less chance of having to do his awful job. On he went, trying to convince himself that he was 'prospecting' for business. The sunlight vanished behind him as he walked deeper and deeper into the forest. Not a house to be seen, until he came to a clearing. There, in front of him, was the strangest house he had ever seen. It was a quaint thatched cottage, which wasn't so much thatched as iced (like a cake that is), and the colours … the door pillars were red and white stripes, the walls were pink, and sort of drippy. Strangest of all were the windows. They seemed to be a patchwork of transparent and semi-transparent stuff. It wasn't glass, it wasn't plastic, it was, well, just stuff! Finally, an opportunity to sell the delights of extruded PVC home improvements.

Derek opened the gate in the small picket fence, which seemed, disconcertingly, to be made of small human bones. He decided that this was unlikely and that it was some kind of trendy garden makeover stunt. The front door was decorated with a brightly painted red gargoyle that, through some clever mechanism like the singing fish thing that everybody gets at Christmas, actually snapped its needle sharp teeth at him and then started yelling, 'There's somebody at the door! There's somebody at the door!'

When the door opened, Derek's breath was taken away as a bent old woman of stunning ugliness stood before him. Should he run? The strategy of running away from faintly dodgy or intimidating customers had always stood him in good stead in the past. No, of course not, this was just a dotty old lady who, with eyes like old hard boiled eggs, would be very unlikely to read his somewhat ambiguous contract.

'Good morning Madam, you have been selected to …'

'How nice,' interrupted the old crone with a very disconcerting smile. One would expect such an elderly, worn-out creature to not have a tooth in her head, but the reverse was the case. In fact she had a lot more teeth than seemed necessary. The thing that spooked Derek was how swiftly and unbidden the word 'shark' sprang to mind.

'Do come in and tell me all about it, we will have a nice hot drink and a sit down so that I can listen to what you have to say.'

Derek's nerves at this point were on the verge of making his legs work like pistons to carry him very swiftly away from this place, but the old lady took his

Notes...

1. The hot drink

The true reason for not accepting a hot drink is that it sets the time agenda. We have a nice quick success, then ... 'Stay and finish your drink!' As we juggle a red-hot polystyrene cup of stuff, and occasionally blowing on it we pass the time of day, 'I'm glad we got this order, things were getting a bit tight after the court case ...'

Try this

'Would you like a drink?'
        'Thank you so much, but I have just had one'.

Then set your own time to perfection.

arm with a vice-like grip. She led him to the kitchen, which was dominated by the largest microwave he had ever seen; it was the size of a telephone kiosk. Unable to think of anything sensible to say, he blurted, 'What a big microwave you have!'

To which she replied, 'All the better to cook … er um ahem,' coughing the last few words into her hand. 'Never mind that, do sit down.'

She placed a steaming cup in front of him and he called to mind the advice in his favourite techniques book *Sell to be Great*, which said, never accept a hot drink from a prospective customer. He had never understood why, until now. Was it that bilious shade of green? Was it the fact that it continued to bubble and steam? No, he decided it was definitely the eye gazing back at him from the frothing liquor that disconcerted him the most.[1]

'OK,' the old lady said, 'what have you got to show me?'

He vaguely remembered that perhaps he should have been asking the questions, but then what did that matter, it was time to start his 'dem' (the demonstration). He had a lovely 'dem', it was like theatre, and it was balletic in its verbal choreography. In short, Derek knew that, given the chance, his dem was irresistible. He got out his sample window. He hit it with his silver hammer to show its unparalleled strength (this, to Derek's horror, produced a hair line crack in the glass, but he was sure the old bat wouldn't notice). He opened it and slammed it to show off the 'Eeezee Glide' hinges. He punctuated every sentence with, 'wouldn't you agree?' just as the book said. He wasn't sure why, but Derek was determined to stick to the script. About a quarter way through, the old woman, who had appeared to be dozing, snapped upright and announced, 'You're pretty crap at this, aren't you?'

Derek was speechless with shock. 'I, er, well, er …,' he looked about in panic, 'It was them, they put me off,' he said pointing outside to the garden.

'Who?'

'Those children, they seem to be eating your roof.'

'Oh them, I blame the parents. You know the little sods roasted my sister, hence the microwave. Anyway, enough of that. Look, your style is so unappetizing, I don't even feel like eat …, um, buying from you.'

'You just didn't give me a chance. No one gives me a chance. Other people have success handed to them on a plate. I struggle and struggle and get nowhere.'

'Would you like to learn the secret of success?' she croaked.

'Of course I want success, but there is nothing I need to learn. I know all there is to know about success, it just eludes me. I tell you, if I had success, I would know what to do with it. I would surprise a few people, I can tell you. I was thinking on the way, if only I had a magic wand I could ...'

'Funny you should say that,' said the old woman producing a sort of metallic, ironish, glowing, wooden stick sort of thing. She waved it and cried, 'Abracadabra!'

'Abracadabra?' said an incredulous Derek.

'The oldies are always the goodies.'

She gave him a huge wink. There was a flash, a thunder crack, and Derek felt very strange indeed.

'Hey, what the ...?' Derek cried out, but his voice was cracking into a throaty growl.

'You need to change your thinking, m'lad. A bit of hard work and humility wouldn't go amiss. A few months, or even years, as a dog will teach you about how to succeed.'

'A dog?' yapped Derek who, by now, was feeling very hairy indeed, 'Months? Years?'

'Come off it, lad, I am supposed to be a wicked witch – what did you expect? Glass slippers and a pumpkin coach? But don't despair, the curse can be lifted.'

'Who have I got to kiss?' panted Derek, who suddenly was horrified to discover that he not only had the desire to nibble his own bottom, but the ability to do so as well.

'Kiss be buggered! You whinged on about success so, when you have the ability to find it and you truly succeed at something then the curse will be lifted.'

The transformation was complete and Derek literally walked out of his suit. He looked towards the front door which seemed to be about thirty feet tall, contemplating his position. He felt a complete prat. He should have noticed the clues: the broomstick, the pointy hat, the 'eye-of-newt' novelty recipe tea towel, or, if nothing else, how the comedy doorknocker had a corresponding red backside with a twitching forked tail. His reverie was interrupted when the door opened of its own accord, and a brightly striped leg terminating in a laced Victorian boot, headed swiftly in his direction.

'Gerrrout of it, you mangy brute,' cried the witch. And Derek was launched into his new life by a swift kick up the arse.

The children in the garden squealed with laughter at the sight of a howling, running border collie wearing nothing but a pair of Calvin Klein underpants. Perhaps they should not have been distracted from their own problem: to wit, a small, wizened old lady who was creeping around the side of the house with a large butterfly net and a copy of Delia Smith.

Derek ran and ran – on all fours, of course. He ran along a street of shops and caught sight of his reflection in a window. No doubt about it, he was a dog, a collie, a sheepdog. What a tragedy, what horror, but didn't the lamp post smell nice, he had never noticed that before. Soon he was back in open country amongst fields and trees, which, to be fair, smelt pretty good too. He decided to whip through a hole in the hedge and into a field to have a bit of a think.

He sat on his haunches to consider his position. Derek had always scratched his ear when he was thinking, but never before with his rear leg.

A big man in a tweedy jacket and a tweedy hat was heading his way. He had big boots and a stick. There was a small man behind him who was just as tweedy but carried a shotgun.

'Help at last,' thought Derek and he rushed up to the men. 'Oh, I am so glad to see you. Please help me, I have been cursed by a wicked witch!'

The big man seemed very angry and shouted at Derek

'Blah, blah, blah, blah! Blah, blah!'

He then gave Derek a mighty crack around the head with his stick.

What Derek hadn't realized was that all the man could hear was, 'Yap, bark, bark, snarl!' – after all, dogs and men don't speak the same language, but that is going to make it very confusing for us – the witnesses of this tale – so from now on we, and only we, will understand both sides.

'It's another of them damn strays, and he looks like a nasty one,' said the smaller man, 'Shall I shoot him?'

'Nah, I'll give him another whack with me stick, then you get a bit of string round his neck. We need another dog. I'll soon whip the sassiness out of him.'

Derek received another mighty whack, and coarse string was pulled tight around his neck. He felt that he was choking and his natural reaction was to pull back. That just made things worse. The string tightened until his eyes bulged and the stick battered him all the more.

'Come on, you brute, it's no good pulling and yapping, we got you!'

At this, the men dragged, kicked, and harried Derek across the fields until they came to a pick-up truck that had a steel cage built on the back. They slung him in it and roared off. Every time the truck cornered, he was hurled from one side to the other, completely unable to keep his footing on the slimy floor, which smelt of every sort of animal dung.

After some time they arrived at Cold Valley Farm, just as dusk was falling.

'Sling him in with the others, I'm going in to get some grub,' the large man snapped before stomping off into the house. The small man roughly dragged Derek to a large, dark-looking shed. Holding him by the scruff of the neck with one hand, he opened the door with the other; Derek was literally picked up and hurled through the air, landing amongst a tangle of hairy legs and snapping teeth. The door slammed shut.

'Oi! Watch it, prat,' came a voice from the gloom.

'Yeah, get out the way if you don't want to lose an ear.'

'Shut up, I'm trying to get some kip.'

As Derek's eyes became accustomed to the gloom, he could make out the shape of a number of other dogs, all collies.

'You the new dog, then, mush?'

'No, I'm a man.'

'A man, eh? You look like a dog to me!'

The speaker was a scruffy collie with a very muscular frame and a mean, sneering expression.

'Not only can I understand what they're saying, but I can also read their expressions,' thought a very confused Derek.

'Eh, Brutus, think it's another tosser been messing with the witch?'

'That's right, short stuff, you been messing with the witch?' asked the snarly dog, who was obviously called Brutus.

'Well, there was an elderly lady in a strange cottage.'

'Yep, you been witched, kid!'

'Have there been others like me? Did they lift the curse, are they still here?'

'They're still here alright. They're on the compost heap – shot and on the compost heap, that's what happens to failures here.'

'Oh, no! How do I avoid being a failure?' pleaded Derek.

'Get him Patch,' snapped Brutus.

Brutus'cohort shot forward and grabbed Derek's throat with his teeth. At this Brutus strolled over and put his face very, very close to Derek's.

'Now listen, pal,' he snarled in a very un-pally way. 'Success is the only thing that matters here. This is an outfit built on success. We are set to be world champions at the sheepdog trials this year. The only thing in our way is the limp-pawed pansies from Sunnydale Farm, and we are going to slaughter them. Now, we are the best, and I am the best of the best. That means I get the easy sheep, the warmest bed, and the best food. So, if you think I'll waste a second of my time on a loser like you, simply to help you to become a rival, you've got another think coming. But if you let us down, you are dead meat. Find success for yourself or watch out for me. Get out of my sight!'

With a vicious twist, Patch let go and Derek limped away into the darkest corner to nurse his wounds.

'Hello mate, you new here?'

Derek noticed a very sly-looking smaller dog.

'Yes, I am. I've been witched apparently.'

'Oh, yeah? Well its crap working here. I'm Dodger by the way. I know how things work, and I can make sure I don't have to work. That is, if I want food, I know where to nick it from. If I want to skive

Notes...

2. The first day at work

What was your first day in a new job like? If you employ people, they are a large investment and their first day can decide whether that investment pays off, or not.

Tips

Make sure they are expected and welcomed. Put them with your best employee (or even you), not your worst. Bad habits are just as easy to learn as good ones.

off, I know where to hide. Don't worry kid, I'll teach you everything you need to know to survive here.'[2]

'Brutus is a bit aggressive.'

'Aggressive? Annoy him and he'll tear your throat out. But, mind you, he is good. He is our star: the best sheepdog in the county and his pal Patch is probably second. They might seem chummy, but they don't trust each other. If Brutus finds a troublesome sheep, he would never warn Patch. Then he laughs when Patch gets into trouble. He says it toughens us up, makes us independent thinkers, capable of standing on our own four paws. Me, I just stay quiet and look after me and, if you've got any sense, you'll do the same. Anyway, time for a bit of kip – busy day tomorrow.'

'Um, where do I, er, kip?' asked Derek.

'Wherever you find a bed, mate.'

'There doesn't seem to be one.'

'Then you will have to push someone out.'

'I can't, that's just …'

'Oh, come on. I'll help you, but only this once and that will be one you owe me. Now let me see, there's Fido the pup, we could intimidate him, but he might snap back and I'm a bit too tired for a fight. Ah! Look, there's Harold.'

Notes...

3.

Is this your environment, 'When the going gets tough, the tough get going', 'Work hard, play hard', 'The fittest survive'.

I have worked in places like this — it doesn't motivate, it <u>discourages</u>.

Derek looked across the shed and there, snuggled mournfully in his bed, was a much older dog with a grey muzzle. He looked at Derek with incredibly sad eyes.

'He's a goner,' said Dodger. 'Old dog and he got injured by a vicious ram. Did his leg in, and it hasn't healed. He's definitely for the compost heap, would have been there now but the farmer didn't want to waste the shotgun cartridge on someone who should have died anyway. We'll get his bed for you.'

With that, Dodger ambled across to the old dog, 'Go on you, clear off! Make room for some new blood, you waste of space.'[3]

Without a sound, the old dog, obviously in pain, dragged himself from his bed. Hauling a clearly useless rear leg, the poor creature made its agonising way to the opening that led to a wire run. As he made his way out, he looked back over his shoulder at Derek with such a look of sad reproach that it tore at his heart.

Derek rushed forward, 'Look, don't leave your bed, I don't mind sleeping on the floor.'

Seconds later he was staring into the snarling face of Brutus. 'You again!' growled the huge dog. 'You must be tired of living. I won't tell you this again, but here, winners are winners, losers are losers. We don't want old gits like him slowing us down. Let him go, or do you fancy your chances against me?'

Derek knew he had no chance against him, but he still went to take a step forward. As he did so, he caught the eye of the old dog, who shook his head in warning and proceeded out into the rain to the far end of the run, where, in dismal resignation, he lay in the mud. Brutus saw Derek step back.

'Smart move, you've just saved your life and learned lesson one. Remember, when you're working here you're not human anymore. It's dog-eat-dog.'

Brutus' snarl turned to a vicious grin and Patch laughed his approval.

As Derek lay on the vacated bed, he decided that he had never felt so alone or miserable in his life. 'Learn the secrets of success,' the witch had said. 'I'll learn nothing in this terrible place,' thought Derek, as he drifted off into a fitful sleep.

A cock crowing woke them the next morning at the crack of dawn, and Derek looked out at the still form of Harold lying in the icy mud. A gate opened. The weaselly, small man appeared and prodded the body with his foot. He shouted, 'Hey boss, Harold's snuffed it. You was right to save your bullet,' and with that, he picked the stiff, bedraggled dog from the mud by his tail and dragged it away in the direction of the compost heap. He was soon back shouting and banging, chasing the dogs into the yard.

Dodger whispered to Derek, 'Keep your head down and stay out of trouble.'

Meanwhile the young pup was getting more excited. It gambolled and yapped and scampered around Derek and Dodger.

'I'm excited and frightened and jumbly inside. It makes my tummy feel really funny,' said the young dog.

Guided by whacks, shouts and curses, the dogs were herded into the brand new shearing shed. It was quite clear whose side Brutus and Patch were on, as they also snapped and growled at any dog that stepped out of line.

'Management lickspittles,' whispered Dodger. 'I'm surprised Brutus' nose isn't as brown as his eyes, its so far up the farmer's ... arrrr owwww!'

'Got a problem, Dodger?' said Patch, through the teeth that were clenched on Dodger's backside.

'No, mate, just showing the new lad the ropes,' squealed Dodger through tears of pain.

'Teaching him to be a lazy git like you, I reck-on.'

They were both distracted by the pup hopping from paw to paw.

Notes...

4.

How does your organization behave when people make mistakes?

'Oh, my belly!'

With that, the young dog rushed into the centre of the immaculate new shed and produced an enormous pooh.

For a moment, there was a stunned silence. The young dog stood frozen, horrified at what he had done. Then all of a sudden, there was an explosion of noise, the dogs were roaring and barking and laughing. The man shouted in fury. The man with the stick flung himself at young Fido.

'You, filthy! Stinking! Disgusting! Creature!'

Each word was punctuated with a vicious blow that made Fido yelp with pain. The yelping seemed to enrage the man more and more, and his blows became frenzied. He beat the dog to the floor, then picked it up and threw it out of the open window.

'Now I've got to clear this mess up. I've had enough of dogs for one day, let's put them back in their shed,' snapped the farmer. The dogs were herded back to the shed and shut in.

Brutus rounded on Fido, 'Well done son, you've dropped us all in it now. Shape up or ship out.'[4]

'But I don't know what they want of me,' whimpered Fido.

'Perhaps not crapping on their new floor would be a good start.'

'I got nervous.'

'Well you had better work out what they do want, before tomorrow.'

The dogs stayed locked in until the morning of the next day when, again, at dawn they were herded to the shearing shed.

Fido was clearly terrified and, to Derek's horror, was starting to hop from paw to paw again. Before anyone could stop him, he rushed forward and, in a repeat of the previous day's performance, produced another huge pooh. This time the thrashing was even more severe, but it ended the same way with Fido being flung through the window.

'Well they ain't getting another day off, work 'em hard while I clear this up,' said the farmer. With that, the weaselly man drove the dogs into a large field where, for the duration of the day, he shouted at them, threw clods of earth at them, and hit them with his stick. Derek had no idea what they wanted him to do, but he seemed to be getting more than his fair share of bruises.

'What do they want me to do?' he asked Patch, as a clod of earth whistled low over his head.

'Learn the job,' snapped back Patch, 'and if you don't learn the job, it will be more than earth and stones heading your way.'

The farmer was standing next to the weaselly man, 'That's enough for one day – get 'em back. What's the new dog like?'

'Rubbish. It just runs about with no idea. If you whack it one, it just runs somewhere else. I feel like killing it half the time.'

'Well, if it doesn't improve, you can. I'm not wasting good food on a waste of space like him.'[5]

The dogs were driven back to the shed, where Derek met Fido licking his numerous wounds.

'You look really beaten up,' said Derek.

'The problem was I just didn't understand what they wanted,' the pup replied.

'It's been agony finding out but I think I have worked out what they expect of me. Just wait until tomorrow – don't worry, I'm sure you'll work it out too.'

The next day dawned and the routine was repeated. As the dogs made their way to the shiny new shearing shed, Fido was clearly shaking with nerves.

Brutus leaned across, 'I hope you've learned your lesson, lad, 'cause we all got a rough time yesterday, thanks to your little performance, I'll tell you. If you think they gave you a thrashing, that'll be nothing compared to what I'll give you.'

Notes...

5.

Make it completely clear what job you expect people to do. If they fail, don't punish but, instead, break the job down into easy stages that they can master and, as they achieve each stage, reward them. This way, people will always feel motivated and that they are achieving something. There is nothing more depressing than a job you don't understand.

'It's OK. I think I understand,' replied the trembling dog.

Once in the shed, Fido was hopping again. Then, all of a sudden, he rushed forward into the middle of the shiny floor where he produced yet another huge pooh, but before anyone could do anything, he jumped out of the window. The farmer rushed to the window and raised the shotgun to his shoulder, but Fido was, by this time, four fields away and still running.

'Won't see him again,' whimpered Dodger to Derek.

The farmer and his nasty little friend were incandescent with fury and gave the dogs (particularly Derek) another harsh, incomprehensible kick. Brutus and Patch, however, seemed to avoid all trouble and, in fact, received high praise for moving smoothly in a pattern that made no sense at all to Derek – but was clearly exactly what the farmer wanted. A number of other dogs were doing enough to avoid trouble while Dodger seemed to be able to become invisible by sneaking about like a shadow. As this went on day after awful day, the more confused Derek became. Then, the fateful day dawned.

'That new dog is useless. It's been here over a week now and he still just runs about whimpering. It's time he went to the compost heap.'

'Yeah, I suppose,' answered the farmer, 'But before we do, let's see how he is with the stock.'

The dogs were led to a field, in the centre of which stood a large ram with curly horns.

'That's Reg, the flock ram,' said Dodger, 'Nasty piece of work he is.'

'It's only a sheep,' said Derek.

'There is sheep, and there is sheep!'

The farmer was whistling and gesticulating at Derek. Seconds later, the customary clod of earth bounced off his head.

'What does he mean?' said a desperate Derek.

Brutus stepped forward. 'OK, just this once I will tell you. We are sheepdogs. That is a *sheep*, ergo you are supposed to herd said sheep. Judging by the farmer's whistles, he wants you to fetch that sheep to him, so look lively'.

'OK, thanks Brutus.'

Derek leapt forward, not noticing Brutus' and Patch's sly exchange of amused glances. He headed out to the centre of the field, where the ram stood. As he got closer, the ram got bigger until he was about ten yards away from the biggest sheep he had ever seen in his life.

'Big or not, it's still only a sheep,' he thought.

At this point, Reg the ram lowered his head and started to move forward. Derek also moved forward, barking to drive the sheep to the farmer.

Reg was gathering speed, a lot of speed, and his hooves started to thunder, making the ground shake. Derek realized the danger he was in, and turned to flee. Too late; it was like being hit by a train.

Derek was flung into the air like a rag toy, the wind completely knocked out of him. He lay on the ground in pain and unable to breathe. He felt the ground thunder again and tried to get up. He was barely on his feet when Reg hit again, and again, and again.

'Get that sheep off him before it damages it- self – valuable ram that,' the farmer shouted. Patch, Brutus, and a group of the experienced dogs, leapt forward at the farmer's whistle. Brutus had no fear of the ram and faced it down with bared teeth. Derek was delighted that the other dogs had saved him.

'One of the group at last,' he thought. Until he saw that they were all backing away from him to a safe distance; until he stood isolated, and alone in the middle of the field. To his horror, he saw the farmer lift the gun to his shoulder. Derek looked for a mi- crosecond down both barrels, then decided to learn Fido's lesson. He was off like the clappers, making for a distant hole in the hedge. He heard the first bang, and the grass sizzled inches from his head. There was a second, and he felt a searing pain as a single pellet passed through his ear. By the time the farmer could reload, Derek had made good his escape.

He ran for miles and miles, until he could run no further. Exhausted, he lay under a bush and slept.

He was woken by a voice. 'Hello boy, you look a bit of a mess.'

He opened his eyes and, to his horror, saw another tough-looking man with a stick – well not a stick as such, more a shepherd's crook – and with him was a very muscular and tough-looking collie sheepdog.

The only odd thing was that he seemed to be able to understand a lot of what the man said.

'You been in the wars, boy?'

The man was gently touching his wounded ear.

'Blow me, another inch to the right and that would have taken your head off. You was real lucky there boy. In fact, what I'm going to do is to call you Lucky. So, Lucky, you going to come with us?'

The man reached for Derek, and he shrank back in fear.

'Had a rough time did you, Lucky? Let me put you with Shep, he will look after you.'

The big dog stepped forward.

'Who did that to you?'

'I was in a terrible place – there were other dogs, terrible men, a shed, and an old dog died. Brutus said ...'

'Brutus? Well, that sounds like you had a spell at Cold Valley Farm. Nasty lot there, but they are our main competitors when it comes to sheepdog trials.'

'Cold Valley Farm is not the only place I had a spell. I'm a man, you know, and it was a spell that made me a dog.'

'Lucky break, that, it's much more fun being a dog. I'd hate to be human,' said the big dog.

'But I like being a human, I want to be one again.'

'And how is that going to happen?'

'I can lift the spell if I can find real success.'

'Well, you have certainly come to the right place. We can turn anyone into a success.'

The big dog beckoned with his head, 'Come on, let's get you back to the farm.'

The shepherd turned to Derek, 'You going to join us, then Lucky? We'd be pleased to have you. I think you are going to be fantastic. I'll put you with

Shep. He's the very best dog and, if you learn what he knows, you could be the best too. So come on, let's get a move on.'

Derek turned to Shep. 'How come I can understand him?'

'Because he has learned to speak our language,' Shep replied.

After a short walk, they crested a hill and came to a farm that was a cliché picture postcard place. The shepherd led the dogs into the yard.

'OK Lucky, I'll leave you with Shep, my very best dog ever, while I take a moment to plan where we start to turn you into the most successful dog ever.'

Then, barking, yapping, jumping, shouting, spinning, leaping, came a familiar figure: it was Fido. The pup had found his way to the same sanctuary. He danced and leapt around and around the shepherd.

'Whoa, boy, steady,' the shepherd laughed at the dog's antics. Then, disaster struck as the young dog's excitement got the better of him and he repeated his pooh-producing party trick. Derek winced, waiting for the explosion of punishment and recrimination, but the shepherd's reaction could not have been more surprising: he bent down and tickled the dog's stomach.

'Well done boy, that's much better than doing it in my nice clean shearing shed. You're a clever dog, and we'll soon have you going out into the field like the other dogs.'

Fido looked into the man's eyes and it was clear that the shepherd had him heart and soul.[6]

Shep turned to the two dogs, 'Come on, follow me, I'll show you where we sleep. You two have got a very busy day tomorrow.'

'Oh, yes?' thought Derek, then turning to Shep he asked, 'What does busy involve?'

'Busy, yes, but it'll be the best day you have ever had. The shepherd has to go to the show tomorrow and it will be a very important day for him. The show is a really exciting place and, as a very special treat or reward, he sometimes takes one or two dogs with him', replied Shep.

'All very interesting, but what happens to us while all this is going on?' Derek asked.

'No, you don't understand, he will take you and Fido with him.'

'Why? What are we being rewarded for?'

'For coming here to work with us. It's so you can understand what we all work together to achieve. We are thrilled that you could join us.'

'What if I fail?'

Notes...
6.

It's a manager's job to catch people doing something right.

'You can't, we won't let you.'

The dogs arrived at a large clean barn that was divided off into stalls for the dogs to sleep in. One was empty and over it was a hand-painted sign bearing the name 'Lucky'. The shepherd's wife had obviously been alerted to their arrival because not only was there a sign but there was also a food bowl, a drinking bowl and a large stuffed cushion, all with 'Lucky' written on them. The food bowl was full of delicious treats, and Derek tucked in. From behind him was uproar and he turned to see a number of other dogs, all cheering and welcoming him. As they were introduced, they all seemed pleased to see him, all except one older dog whose name was Butch. He viewed Derek with suspicion.

'Come on Butch, welcome the new lad,' Shep said.

'Harrumph! I'll wait until he proves himself,' said Butch, as he stalked off to his bed.

'OK lads, turn in, very busy day tomorrow,' called Shep to all the dogs.

The next day, Derek was woken by the shepherd coming into the barn.

'Come on Fido, come on Lucky, into the truck, boys.'

To Derek's surprise, they were allowed in the cab where it was warm.

What a day they had. The shepherd took them to a place of sights and smells, where they were given treats and fuss that almost sold Derek on the idea of staying a dog. More to the point, he was able to see what a valuable and important job he would be expected to do. It was late when they returned, and Derek was the living cliché of 'tired, but happy'.

'Here are your new boys, Shep,' said the shepherd. 'Let them get some kip – the real work starts tomorrow.'

'OK,' said Shep. 'Let's you and I sit together, Lucky, and we can agree exactly what your job is, what you need to learn to succeed, and how we can measure when you have succeeded.'

Derek listened intently to the other dog.

'Our job description, if you like, is to be sheep-dogs or, in other words, to move sheep under our complete control from one place to another. Each time we encounter an obstacle, we should be able to take the sheep around, through, or over it, without giving them any distress. We should stay in complete control until the sheep reach their destination.'

'What does the shepherd do?'

'Well, although he or she is *ipso facto* the boss, their real job is to do everything they can to enable us to do our job. Things like opening gates, etc. Of course it is they who decide the destination for the sheep, but that is agreed with us long before we start to move the sheep. OK, I don't want you to be worried or upset, but just so I can see what you *do* know, let's give you a try. Feel alright?'[7]

'Yes, raring to go!' Derek felt very confident about this sheep herding business – he was sure that his skill as a human salesman would stand him in good stead.

'Now, the first thing you need to know about sheep is …,' started Shep. But his words blew away uselessly in the wind as Derek set off at a blistering pace. In the distance he could see a small herd of the hairy little gits, so he tore at them barking and yelping with new found confidence. The creatures looked up from their quiet grazing, somewhat startled by this crazy barking apparition.

'Stand and fight, or run,' was the herd's thought. The speed, the barking, the exuberance decided them: they scattered, running and leaping in all directions.

Derek had got the idea that it would be best to bring them in together and, at that moment in time, together they were not. Derek always admired tough

Notes...

7. Shepherd/boss

Even when we trust our team to do a great job, it really helps when we use our power and status to open gates for them.

role models and he pictured the craggy-chinned, iron-haired American general that he had seen on TV. 'That could be me,' thought Derek.

'Yep, that's right,' he thought, tightening his jaw, 'It's round-up time!'

But the more he tried to herd them, the more they scattered, and they didn't do their scattering in abject terror either; some were quite sassy and turned to threaten him with – what was unusual for sheep – some very sharp looking horns. Derek decided that he should cut his losses and just bring one back and, as luck would have it, he cornered one of the creatures. In seconds, however, the tables had turned and the trapped animal, its head lowered, started to gather speed in Derek's direction. Derek's experience with the ram had taught him what to expect. He turned and fled, and the impact, when it came, though painful, mostly speeded him back down the field to Shep. When he arrived, Shep had the doggy equivalent of a wry smile on his face.

'Good try, Lucky, but ...'

'Don't tell me, I know, I'm rubbish. I'm always rubbish – what sheepdog gets chased by sheep?'

'No, don't beat yourself up. The enthusiasm was there, the energy was there, the effort was there, but it was wasted effort.'

Notes...

8.

If you want sheep, don't waste your time herding goats. To use a very ancient sales phrase, be prepared to 'qualify' your customers. Question them of course, but this may be misleading. People don't like to admit that they are goats, so look for clues and ask indirect questions.

'Are you interested in exotic holidays and fine wines?'

'Yep.'

'As a matter of interest, what do you drive and which is your favourite TV show?'

'Um, a 1994 Nissan Sunny and I like Neighbours.'

Not conclusive, but it does suggest a touch of goatiness!

'Well the sheep weren't very easy. How could I have done better?'

Shep nodded sagely, 'Well first of all, they weren't sheep.'

'Not sheep?'

'No, they were goats. Don't waste your time chasing goats. We don't want the goats.'

'Well they look like sheep,' said Derek defensively.

Shep smiled.[8]

'I take your point. It can be difficult to tell the sheep from the goats, so we must be careful to use a series of tests to satisfy ourselves that they are not goats. For instance, you could ask them questions.'

'Brilliant idea,' cried Derek, and he tore off towards another crowd of hairy creatures, approaching what appeared to be the lead animal, who was thoughtfully chewing a thistle.

'Are you sheep,' he asked.

'Yep,' the animal replied.

'I've got to herd some sheep soon. Would you be interested?' Derek asked eagerly.

'Delighted, mate,' replied the hairy animal.

'Would you like to be herded now?'

'Give it a moment, old son, I'll just have to clear it with the others – who, as you can see, are a bit busy at the moment.'

Derek looked around, 'busy' seemed to consist of a lot of communal thistle chewing, but who was he to argue? As they say, 'The customer is always right'.

'So, when would you see yourselves being herded?'

'Oooh, I don't know. Come back in an hour or two or, better still, we'll bleat when we need you.'

At this, the creature just fell silent and stared at Derek. This made Derek feel very uncomfortable and gave him the irresistible desire to say something.

'Oh, um, that's great then, um, I'll pop back later and … or … wait here or … wait to hear from you then.'

'You do that, son.'

'Well, nice to have met you.'

Derek scampered back to Shep, full of excitement.

'There you go, Shep, my first bit of herding.'

'Well done – you're doing a great job, and it took a lot of nerve asking complete strangers questions, but did you feel that you managed to herd them very far?'

'Well, I'm sure I did herd them quite a bit.'

'I'm sure you did, but when I do it, I like to be sure that I have achieved some measurable success, so I like to know how far I have moved them.'

'Well, you can see how far I moved them!' yapped Derek, pointing with his paw.

'I grant you they do look a bit moved, but where were they before you moved them?'

'A long way from there,' declared Derek.

'In the right or wrong direction?' asked Shep. 'Before we start herding, we need to be sure where exactly the sheep are.'

'How?'

'One method is to ask the sheep themselves. I call those, "position questions".'

'I asked them questions and they told me they were very interested in being herded,' said Derek proudly.

'They told you they were sheep as well, did they?'

'Yep, and once they've finished what they're doing, I've got to pop back and they'll let me take them to the pen.'

'That sounds great, but I've got a nasty feeling that they are goats.'

'Goats!' Derek's jaw dropped. 'But they said they were sheep.'

Notes...

9.

In all sizes and types of sales it is important to use positional questions — as Shep said, people don't feel threatened when talking about the past.

'Did you have a holiday last year?'
'Yes.'
'Where did you go?'
'Spain.'
'Oh, Spain. Did you enjoy it?'
'Yes, very much.'
'So, Spain again?'
'No, but we would like the same sort of weather.'

This could go on for some time, but you can see that until you know where they are, you won't be able to tell where they are going.

'Goats tend to do that. They get embarrassed if folk think they're not up to being sheep.'

'There wasn't much point in asking them if they were sheep, then?' said Derek, feeling that he had been had.

'I agree, asking direct questions doesn't always get you very far, but come on Lucky, you're a very clever dog – after all, you used to be human. Think about it, ask indirect questions that are guided by your intuition. You don't want to trap or embarrass them, talk about the past. No one minds talking about the past, and it gives a great idea of the future.'[9]

Before things could go any further, there was uproar from the field next door – one that did not belong to their farm. There was furious barking, shouting and bleating. Shep and Derek rushed to the hedge to see what was going on. Derek gaped at the sight that met his eyes. Large wolf-like dogs were pursuing hundreds of, clearly, terrified sheep. Teeth bared, the savage brutes cannoned into their hapless prey. Any sheep that resisted would be bitten or charged down.

'Are they wolves?' whispered Derek hoarsely.

'No, they're sheepdogs too,' answered Shep grimly, obviously not liking what he was seeing.

'Sheepdogs? Like us?' Derek was incredulous, but secretly a bit admiring of the powerful savagery of the big dogs.

'No, not like us. They are called German shepherds and they work for the abattoir – the slaughterhouse to you and me. It's their job to get those sheep on that lorry. They can be as tough and as vicious as they like, because those sheep are never coming back. You would probably call their methods "high pressure".'

'Why can't we be a bit tougher? They are certainly achieving their goals.'

'You see, there are two ways of making a living from sheep – and make no mistake, that's what we're here for, making a living off sheep. The first way is to kill the sheep, skin it, and sell the meat for pies, the bones for glue, and the hide for leather. You will make a living but, let me ask you this, how often can you skin a sheep?'

'Umm,' Derek thought for a moment. 'Only once?'

'Correct, only once.'

'Now believe it or not,' Shep smiled. 'Some of the sheep actually like me. I have worked with the older ones for years and, because I have never hurt or taken advantage of them, they trust me. In other words, we have a relationship of trust.'

'How does that make a living?' Derek asked.

'Because with love, attention and trust, one hot day the sheep will sidle up to that trusted figure and say, "Baah, it ain't half hot in this fleece," and I reply that I can help with that. If they would like to just wait in the pen, I can get the farmer to shear that hot old wool off them. Lucky, how many times can you shear a sheep?'

'Lots?'

'That's right, lots!'[10]

'So, I just need to build a relationship with the sheep over time, so they trust me and put themselves in the pen?' said Derek.

'No, that's just a bonus. The new sheep don't know me and need to be firmly controlled throughout the herding process. But I do respect them and I have their best interests at heart. After time, they trust me and join the growing band of sheep who are easy to do business with, because we have a relationship of trust.'

'Growing band?'

'Yes, finding and keeping profitable sheep is the name of the game. I don't think I have ever lost a sheep – except to old age – and, of course, there

Notes...

10.

This book uses the allegory of a sheepdog's journey with the sheep to make us think of our journey with the customer, but does it mean from when a first contact is made to the closing of the sale? Or does it mean from the first contact to the entire life of the customer. Finding and keeping customers is the only activity that generates money; everything else generates cost.

Why do your customers' journeys end and who was involved? Perhaps everyone in your organization should take responsibility for making the relationship last forever.

is the relationship of trust with my fellow dogs. We help each other and can look after each other's sheep – with no fear on either side. It's called working as a team but, to do that, you have to share the rewards.'

Derek's attention was drawn back to the German shepherds. Although they worked vigorously with a kind of violent energy, and even snapped at each other, there was symmetry to the way they worked; if a sheep broke loose, two or even three dogs would work in unison until the terrified creature was brought under control.

'What motivates them?' Derek asked.

'The more sheep they bring in, the better they are fed. No sheep, no food.'

'That's like Brutus and his mates. Every dog for themselves,' said Derek.

'Not quite, they're not as stupid as that. In fact, they are very clever dogs. It's not a cleverness that I can admire, but they are intelligent enough to realize that when a new dog starts with them, it is necessary to let them have a few easy sheep, or they become demoralized. They also work together when they have to.'

'So, in a way, then, they are a team?' Derek observed.

Notes...

11.

You could be as high pressure as the slaughterhouse dogs but, like them, don't expect to see your customers again, <u>ever</u>.

'No! They are not a team, they are a pack – and there is an enormous difference.'

Derek noticed that one of the sheep had managed to get a prickly hedge between itself and the slaughterer's lorry.

'That's a pretty insurmountable obstacle,' Derek remarked.

'We'll see,' Shep replied.

The sheep tried to break free, but the wolf-like dog was too quick; it charged in, teeth bared. The sheep's other choice was to turn and fling itself at the prickly hedge. The creature became a tangled mass of thrashing legs, wool, and twigs.

The huge yellow-eyed dog stood patiently until the sheep untangled itself, and then it charged again. This happened time and time again, until the sheep eventually tumbled over to the other side of the hedge.

'Well he certainly overcame that obstacle.'

'He may have done, but his sheep is exhausted and terrified. He will have to drive on with that level of aggression until the bitter end, which will leave both sheep and dog completely exhausted – and, let me tell you, the sheep will never want to repeat that experience,' said Shep.

'He won't get a chance to,' declared Derek.

'Fair point,' said Shep, grimly.[11]

'We must encounter obstacles. I know I did when I was human, and without a bit of push and shove, all was lost.'

'There is a better way, and you will learn it when the time is right,' said Shep.

It wasn't long before most of the sheep were on the lorry, all of them bleating with upset and terror; but, just as it looked like everything was over, an enormous furore started. The pack had closed in on one last animal. There was a snarling and a snapping, with wool and fur flying in all directions. For a moment, a space cleared and Derek saw that the centre of attention was Reg, the ram. Reg was a clever sheep and he knew only too well what was going to happen to him. Reg was fighting for his life. Down went his head, and he charged again and again. Derek could hear the cracks and bangs as Reg's horns struck home. He knew how tough Reg could be under normal circumstances, but now he was desperate and Derek doubted that even these viciously strong dogs could subdue him. However, each time a dog was flung aside another and another would pile in, until even Reg became exhausted and the pack drove closer and closer to the lorry, with the brave ram fighting every inch of the way. Finally the tailgate was lifted into place and locked.

As the lorry moved away, the dozens of frightened eyes looking out of the lorry, taking their final journey, haunted Derek. He hated and feared Reg, but for such a brave animal to end like that quite upset him. As the lorry accelerated out of the field, it created a huge fog of dust and, as it settled, Derek saw a battered and defiant figure – torn and bleeding, but still standing. It was Reg, a fact that the pack hadn't failed to notice. This time they closed in for the kill. There was no way that Reg was going to survive this. The pack's human was furious.

'That vicious old ram 'as got back off the lorry, would you believe it?' he shouted to his pal. Then, to the dogs, 'OK then, finish him.'

It was at this point that Shep and Derek's shepherd stepped in.

'Whoa there, Frank! He's worth nothing to you if they tear his throat out.'

'Yep, but it'd be a lesson to any other ram who gets ideas above his station. Shame really, he'd be a fine ram if you could control him.'

'I'll take him off your hands,' the shepherd said, and waved a few bank notes under the man's nose.

The man grabbed them. 'OK, mate, he's yours, and good luck.'

The shepherd put a rope around Reg's neck; the ram tried to fight but just didn't have the strength.

'He might have had the stuffing knocked out of him for now, but when he's recovered, I bet we'll meet him again,' thought Derek with a shiver.

They turned away from the hedge. In one of the sun-lit meadows stood a group of woolly animals.

'Now,' said Shep, 'I'll give you a little help. Those are definitely sheep and they definitely need herding, but …'

'You don't need to tell me twice,' and, with that, Derek shot off like a rocket. He had been a little scared and intimidated by the savage German Shepherds, but they had succeeded in everything they attempted (well nearly everything, except for terrible old Reg), so he couldn't help but admire them. Perhaps, he should take a leaf from their book: forceful; aggressive; positive. That's where he had been going wrong. He had let people (and sheep and goats and other dogs) walk all over him. Well, it was no more Mr Nice Guy – um … dog.

He blazed into the group of sheep, barking like a mad thing. The sheep looked up from their quiet grazing with horror at this galloping, noisy apparition. Seconds later they had scattered, bleating in terror, but, unlike the goats, Derek could keep small groups together by intimidation. Once he had got a few sheep together, he chased them hither and thither. 'This is the life,' he thought, 'I am in control now.'

The only problem seemed to be that no sooner had he got a group of sheep where he wanted them, he would turn round to find all the others had scattered. But no worries, at least he was doing some real herding with a respectable collection of sheep. So what if he missed a few – a hit rate of 15% was pretty good. He herded them this way and that way, then that way and this way, and that way, then that way, and this way, but after a while, he began to tire and quite obviously so were the sheep. In fact they were becoming quite distressed with their tongues lolling and panting like bellows.

'Enough herding for one day,' he decided, and trotted back to Shep.[12]

Strangely, Shep was looking less than pleased.

'Lucky, you are a very likeable fellow, and I am so pleased that you have decided to join our team. Your energy and enthusiasm is a real asset and that makes you very important to me.'

Derek glowed, but not for long.

'That is why,' Shep continued, 'I was so disappointed to see that awful display just then. First, what were you doing?'

Notes...

12.

If you rush your customers, they will run away.

'Herding!'

'Where did you learn to "herd" with such violence?'

'The German Shepherds, they kept control.'

'With vicious, unpleasant, high-pressure methods. Look at your sheep.'

Derek turned. The sheep were still trembling, looking at him with fear and loathing.

'Do you think they want to repeat that experience? Have you got a relationship with them? You may never be able to work with these sheep again. Do you agree?'

'Yes, I suppose.' Derek felt awful.

'And where were you herding them to?'[13]

'Herding them to?' This hadn't occurred to Derek.

'Do you know that is such a typical human trait: herding with no idea of where or why. You get up every day and expend huge amounts of energy with absolutely no goal or objective. Look, we are simple dogs, and you have seen sheepdogs working, have you ever seen a dog herding sheep with absolutely no idea where to herd them to?'

'No.' Derek hung his head. He had never felt more depressed. Now he had even managed to upset his hero, Shep.

Notes...

13.

Before we even think of approaching people, just take a few moments to decide what exactly you want to achieve, and where you would like them to be when you have finished.

'Well, end of lecture,' Shep's eyes sparkled again. 'I bet you won't make these mistakes again. I feel responsible for not explaining things carefully enough. So, what do you say, we'll work together, and I will show you the best way. Together we will make you the biggest success in sheep dogging.'

'When do we start?' Derek was excited again.

'Soon, but first I'd better go and apologize to the sheep, and try and set things straight,' said Shep.

'Why should you apologize?' gasped Derek. 'It was me who chased them and upset them.'

'I know, but you are part of my team and I should take full responsibility. Always take responsibility when dealing with those who have been upset, it makes it easier.'

'I can do that,' said Derek eagerly.

'I'm glad to hear that, but for now, come along and watch me.'

Shep approached the sheep, who watched him with a great deal of suspicion.

'I'm sorry to bother you,' said Shep to the sheep, 'but I just saw what happened during the herding.'

'Yeah, baa, awful, baa! Disgraceful, baa, shouldn't be allowed, baa!'

Shep held up his paw and the sheep stopped bleating for a moment.

Notes...

14.

When you have to apologize or deal with a complaint, say that you are sorry and accept full responsibility, no matter whose fault you might think it was. That way three things happen:

- the customer accepts what you say;
- they respect you; and
- they understand.

Before your lawyers start, you can be responsible without being liable. You can be sorry that they are disappointed, without you being the one that disappointed them.

'And I have just come to say … I am so sorry, I have completely ruined your day and I'm sorry.'

There was a long silence and after a bit of thought, a bewildered sheep said, 'Well, it wasn't your fault.'

Shep replied, 'That's very kind of you to be so understanding, but I am responsible for the behaviour of my team member and I am so sorry that I have let you down. So, what can I do to put this right for you?'

Soon the sheep were chatting away to Shep in a very relaxed manner and to Derek's amazement their anger had completely evaporated.

Shep left the sheep with a cheery comment and returned to Derek's side.[14]

'That was amazing, you had them eating out of your hand. But why did you take the blame? When I was human, I always used to get customers whinging at me for things that weren't my fault, stuff that the fitter hadn't fitted properly, or things that the truck drivers had broken. In fact, the whole of the head office was a shambles. I never got paperwork, the wrong stuff was delivered, and then the customers would have a go at me. Well, I was on their side – and I would tell them what a useless load of idiots I worked for.'

Notes...

15.

Have a clear view of the whole job: warts, obstacles, distance, and all. Most of all, don't fool yourself.

'And this made the customers happier?' Shep enquired.

'Um, no, to be fair, it enraged them.'

'Look, if you accept full responsibility you win status, respect, understanding and acceptance.'

'Yes, but to those sheep you are important.'

Shep smiled, 'I appear important *because* I take responsibility. Talking of responsibility, I am responsible for turning you into a fully functioning successful sheepdog, so come on, let's learn the right way to do it.'

Shep took Derek to a grassy knoll that overlooked a group of meadows in which a group of unsuspecting sheep were grazing.

'To help you get started,' said Shep, 'I can, once again, assure you that what you see there are definitely sheep, and they most certainly need herding. Now, this is a great place to start from because it will give us a clear view of the whole job, and also some idea of the obstacles we are likely to encounter.'[15]

Derek sat next to Shep and joined him in scanning the area in view.

Shep continued, 'There is the pen that we need to get them into, and that is our goal. When the sheep are safely penned in there, we have succeeded. Go and meet the sheep, and see how well you get on with herding them. You can see where they are; you know they are sheep; you know they need herding; and you can see the pen. Now off you go!'

Derek ran off down the hill but, as he neared the sheep, he slowed so as not to spook them.

'Oh, hi sheep! Let me introduce myself, I'm Derek the new sheepdog. Round here they call me Lucky (actually when I was human, I was called Derek)!'

This time Derek was certain he hadn't frightened the sheep, in fact they seemed very unruffled indeed. One or two looked up still thoughtfully chewing.

'Oh, yeah, hi Lucky', bleated one. 'Yeah, hi Lucky,' bleated another. There was a moment when all you could hear was munching grass. Derek felt a bit uneasy. A large sheep, feeling Derek's embarrassment, broke the silence.

'Yeah, OK, now we've met, what do you want?'

'Well, first let me say thank you for seeing me. I can see you are all so busy grazing and I won't take too much of your valuable time. I just want to tell you about a marvellous opportunity you all have. There's a pen, just two fields away, please feel free to shut yourselves in it, or if I could help in any way, just bleat if you need anything.'

'Yes, sounds great,' said the sheep. 'Thank you for letting us know, Lucky'.

'Could you see yourselves getting moving soon?' asked Derek.

'Yep, could be. We are certainly interested in grazing somewhere different, so thanks for your time. Look, we don't want to be rude, but we really must be getting on with things here.'

Derek stood for a while, not knowing what to do next.

'Er, OK, I expect you need to think things over then?'

'Think things over, yeah, that's what we'll do, we'll think things over,' replied the sheep.

'I'll be off then,' said Derek.

'Yes, you get off then,' said the sheep.

As Derek left, the sheep called after him, 'We are interested!'

Derek heard the sheep say, 'Nice friendly dog, that.'

And he thought to himself, 'Nice friendly sheep, there.'

He returned to Shep feeling quite pleased with himself. What was it he was trying to remember from his commercial life? Yes, that was it: he was building a great relationship with those sheep.

Notes...

16.

However friendly the interchange, if no measurable progress was made, it was still a failure.

'How did you get on?' asked Shep.

'Brilliant,' replied the excited Derek. 'The sheep were really interested.'

'So you got them in the pen then?'

'Well ... not actually in the pen, *per se*.'

'OK, you got them out of the field they're in, then?'

'No.'

'So, what did you achieve?'

'Well, I've got a great relationship with them,' Derek said proudly.[16]

'That's great, but we have a job to do and that job is to move the sheep from where they are, to where they need to be,' said Shep.

'But the sheep aren't ready to move yet. I think, if I pushed them, I would upset them and spoil the relationship. The problem is they seem quite happy where they are.'

'Well, there you have the first obstacle to overcome. The sheep are happy where they are and you need to move them. However kind, however gentle, however understanding we are, our job is to go out there and bring about a change in the current situation. Everyone, especially sheep, is resistant to change so, however careful we are, we will probably start off by getting sheep (or people) to do things they don't want to do. Come on! Let's look at the task again.'

Shep led Derek to the top of the knoll again. When Derek looked down, he could see how far the sheep were from the pen and how many obstacles there were in the way. His optimism vanished like smoke as the true difficulty of the task came home to him.

'It's so easy to fool yourself when you are not really getting anywhere,' Derek thought to himself, and he immediately became depressed.

Shep noticed Derek's downcast expression.

'Why so glum?'

'Well I have done the "V. interested" thing all my life, and the customers, or, if you like, the sheep, have always played along. I was happy to be fobbed off and they were happy to fob as long as they didn't have to move. Look, I can see how difficult it is now. Can I have some easier sheep with fewer obstacles?'

'If I had them, of course you could,' Shep replied. 'But life's not like that. There is the job, there is the distance, and those are the obstacles. For now, just the fact that you can clearly see the task is a great step forward so, to start with, why don't we return to the farm, have a bit of grub, and then come back with the other dogs, and we will make it a bit of a team effort. You will soon learn the other secrets of success.'

'Other secrets?' gasped Derek. 'I don't think I know *any* of the secrets of success yet.'

'I think you do. Just a few more hints and tips and you will never fail.'

Derek trotted along with Shep, feeling a lot better. As they crested the hill, there was uproar in the farmyard, with barking, yelping, clouds of dust, and lots of noise. All the fuss was about a long piece of wood, with two dogs pulling one end and Fido, the young pup, pulling on the other. Although they seemed to be enjoying it, Fido was definitely coming off the worst. Shep rushed forwards.

'Uh oh, here's trouble,' Derek thought. But, to his amusement, Shep joined in on Fido's side. Soon there was a huge amount of uproar and good-natured growling as Shep helped Fido to get the upper paw.

'Don't just stand there gawping,' said one of the other dogs through clenched teeth, 'give us a hand, Lucky.'

'Oh well,' thought Derek, 'in for a penny ...,' and he was soon growling and tugging with the others but, out of the corner of his eye, he saw the shepherd coming.

Notes...

17.

Have fun!

'What on earth is all this noise?' the man shouted. But, by his smile, it was obvious that he wasn't really cross. He grabbed the stick in the middle and tried to outpull all the dogs, and then he started to turn faster and faster until the dogs feet left the ground; but still they hung on. The man soon tired and stopped. He mopped his sweating face with a huge red handkerchief. The dogs dropped the stick and watched, their heads tilted, ready for fun.

'Now, come on lads, you win. You tired me out!' but no sooner had the words left the farmer's mouth than Fido ran forward, grabbed the handkerchief in his mouth, and set off with it at a gallop. As the shepherd chased after him, Shep barked with laughter and excitement. Finally, things cooled off and Fido dropped the handkerchief at the shepherd's feet.

'You scoundrels,' he said in a friendly voice, as he went back into the farmhouse still mopping his brow with what was a very soggy, chewed, red rag.

'That was fun,' laughed Shep. 'There you are, Lucky, another lesson in success, have fun.'[17]

'But don't you get distracted thinking about the work?' asked Derek.

'When I'm not doing the job and I am having fun, I'm having fun – that's it, full stop. After all, I'm a dog. I don't worry. No work, then I have fun, or I eat, or I sleep. It's something that you humans would do well to learn: to separate the bits of life so they don't interfere with each other. Of course, on the other hand, when I do my work, I give one hundred per cent of my mind to the job.'

'How do you learn to do that? I think there is still enough human in me that prevents me being able to do that.'

'I'm not into the mind things, but there is a guy who could help,' said Shep, nodding across the yard. There, in a patch of warm sun, lay the farm's huge ginger tomcat. Some strange feeling, that came from deep inside, grasped Derek. A red mist arose round him. 'Cat!' he thought. 'Must chase cat.'

Shep saw the look in Derek's eyes and it was a look he had seen many times before.

'I wouldn't if I was you, Lucky …,' was all Shep could belatedly suggest, but it was to no avail: Derek set off snarling.

Now, Herbert (for that was the cat's name) had just enjoyed a good lunch of well matured scraps from the kitchen pedal bin and was restfully digesting them. He had insides that would shame a chemical works. The sun had done two jobs: it had relaxed him to the point of making him almost boneless, like a huge soft pyjama case; and it had also brought his digestive system nicely to working temperature. So, as he slowly breathed, he produced clouds of smelly wind from an aperture furthest from the one used for breathing. In other words: he smiled, he relaxed, and he farted.

This whole vision somehow enraged Derek and he rushed indignantly to attack. The other dogs looked away, not wanting to see what they knew was coming next. Derek was a hair's breadth from this evil-smelling soft toy when, in a blink of an eye, it disappeared. A split second later, the air was torn by a savage hiss and a howling noise that was so terrifying it could freeze a person's blood. Something fell on Derek's head, something large, warm, and suffocating. Was it the cat? But this thing was not soft, it was muscular, fast moving and had sharp, pricking, cutting, scratching, tearing bits everywhere. To Derek, it was as if he had stuck his head in a thundercloud. Moments later it was over, before Derek had even thought of defending himself – let alone trying to. Battered, scratched and bewildered, Derek looked around. To his surprise, in a patch of sun some way away, lay the cat – just as relaxed as it had been. The only clue that it might have been the source of Derek's pain was an occasional angry twitch of the last inch of this monster's tail.

The look on Shep's face at Derek's return said it all. If it was possible for a dog to raise its eyebrows, Shep did it then.

'What I meant was, watch him, not attack him,' Shep said. 'Let me ask you, before that regrettable incident, what was that cat doing?'

'Well, apart from farting, I suppose nothing.'

'A cat doing nothing.'

'Yep, a cat doing nothing.'

Derek heard a scurrying and, out of the corner of his eye, there was a sudden and very fast movement. A rat! Or was it? The movement had stopped behind a log. Yes! It was a rat that shot at terrific speed to a new hiding place.

Shep nudged Derek and pointed with his long nose towards the sleeping cat. Only the cat wasn't sleeping, it was crouching, its wide open eyes burned with a terrifying green fire, and Derek could see that the once soft furry bag was a mass of taut muscles, like a coiled spring. Although these muscles seemed to ripple, the cat was, in fact, completely still. Just its mouth seemed to move a little, as it tasted the air and gave words of encouragement, 'Oh yes, come on, move, run, just another tiny step'. It was a killing machine. Derek asked himself with horror how he had ever been stupid enough to even think about attacking this monster.

'What is the cat doing at this exact moment?' asked Shep.

'Well, not a lot. Well, nothing really,' Derek replied hesitantly.

'That's what you said he was doing when he was lying in the sun.'

'Yes, I know, but I suppose there are two sorts of doing nothing.'

'Two sorts of doing nothing? I have seen humans when they talk. If one is bored or distracted, it is as if they are not even there. Don't you humans have an expression "miles away"? Well, that's not our way. When we are here, we are here. As you saw, when we have fun, we have fun. Humans get all mixed up. They stress about work when they should be resting or having fun, then, when they do work, they do it with half a brain or less and they are surprised when they fail.'

The cat was disturbed by the conversation and he glared at the dog.

'If looks could kill – now I know where that expression came from,' thought Derek.

The farmyard fell completely silent. The cat settled, its paws forward, its claws flexing in the dust like

Notes...

18.

When you are involved with people, family, friends, and customers give one hundred per cent of your attention. Be there for them.

a gun-slinger's fingers. There was a flash of movement from behind an old can. Bang! There was a ginger streak, an explosion of claws, teeth, and vigorous movement, and it was game over for the rat.

'One hundred per cent attention – he never fails. That rat was dead the minute he showed his face in the yard. Remember, when your mind starts to wander, think "Farting cat",' said Shep.[18]

He then turned to the other dogs, 'OK, gang, it is time to herd sheep.' And to Derek, 'Now to have some fun – you are going to learn how to do it.'

The group of dogs arrived looking at the grassy knoll where the shepherd was already waiting for them. Shep and the other dogs sat next to him. They waited patiently but Derek could feel the pent-up energy just as he had seen in the cat.

'Are you ready, Lucky?' asked the shepherd. 'Don't worry, you follow Shep, you won't go far wrong.' The shepherd let out a piercing whistle and shouted, 'Go on!'

The dogs shot forward as one, Derek along with them. He had never felt that he belonged more at any time in his life – dog or human.

'Stay by me and don't do anything unless I say,' said Shep.

The dogs circled round in a wide arc, while a couple broke away and moved ahead of where the sheep were expected to go. Shep shot forward and closed in on the sheep. Derek noted that a few of them were the sheep that had given him the brush-off earlier. As Shep closed in, the sheep became restless but Shep's approach, although firm and positive, was in no way aggressive. Nonetheless it became obvious to the sheep that they would feel more comfortable if they moved, which they did with a fair bit of bleating and complaining, but no sense of panic or fear.

'It doesn't look as though you are making too many friends,' panted Derek, as he tried to keep pace with Shep.

'It's that initial resistance – you have to over-come it,' Shep replied. 'It is the great dilemma in herding. Keep that marvellous relationship, don't push the sheep, leave them alone and they stay where they are. Fine, but we need them to be somewhere else. Everyone dislikes change and, if it is your job to bring about change, then you will have to deal with a bit of resistance.'

Derek noted that the sheep were trundling along quite swiftly and Shep was starting to back off.

'Look!' said Shep. 'The sheep are quite happy now. They think they are running where they want to go, which, as it happens, is away from us, which is also, as it happens, towards where we want them to be. The trick is to stay in control but with such a light touch that no one spots it. That means very careful planning. You must always give the impression that the other party is using their free will.'[19]

Derek felt he was getting the hang of this herding game and he moved ahead of Shep. One of the rear sheep glanced around, saw Derek and immediately panicked. It tried to run away from this pounding, eager dog. Having nowhere to go, it ran bleating into the sheep in front, knocking its head sideways but still it pressed on. This set the others off and they tried to climb over each other in their eagerness to escape their tormentor. It was a stampede.

'Lie down now!' hissed Shep to Derek, who was so upset by his blunder that he immediately obeyed. Shep lay down beside him and, in a weird sort of way, seemed quite relaxed.

'Nice weather we are having for the time of year,' Shep said.

'Hey?' replied an amazed Derek.

'I said, nice weather. I do believe I saw a young turtle dove in that thicket over there.'

'Hey?' repeated Derek.

Notes...

19.

When things look as though they are going well, stay cool. If you push, you could blow it. If you back off too much, you can also blow it. Use your doggy head — be attuned to the panic emotion of the other party.

'Look, I think I have taken enough of your time. Let me leave you with this for now and we will get together again. Shall we say next week, or would the week after be better for you?'

Backing off but still in control, still on the journey.

Things slowing, heels dragging?

'That's about everything. May I suggest we move things forward by you taking the first order now, and I will follow up in a day or two to see how you get on.'

The sheep thundered on but stopped short when the lead dogs, standing fast and firm, blocked their way, with their heads lowered, right in the sheep's path. The sheep turned to see which was more frightening: the dogs ahead or their savage pursuers. To their amazement, all they saw behind them were two very relaxed dogs enjoying the sun. The sheep very soon calmed down, and it wasn't long before they had got back to grazing.

'I'm so sorry,' said Derek. 'I cocked it up again.'

'No damage done, Lucky,' said Shep. 'You are doing a great job and it's a mistake we all make from time to time. When things get moving, we are tempted to overdrive them, to push on too hard at a pace that the other party is not ready for, so they panic. But look at them now that we have lost all forward movement. The exact pace is the key to success: too slow, and momentum is lost; too fast, and we generate panic and resistance.'

'I see that,' said Derek, 'but how do you tell the right speed?'

'Experience, of course, but you can also get clues. Remember that farting cat? Be there one hundred per cent. Taste the air. Listen to the sheep's conversation. Are they experiencing worries? Remember, you can't

Notes...

20.

In the old days, this was called 'Dealing with objections', but now that we partner our customers, we should look at these as 'concerns'. We should look for signals: 'Under the circumstances' is a classic signal. They are not saying, 'No, no way'; they are suggesting that, if the circumstances were different, there would be a way. Listen for, 'At these prices, we couldn't', 'Unless you are prepared ...', 'Considering our past experiences ...', 'I don't see how at the moment'.

We listen to concerns and, together with the customers, we put their minds at ease.

herd worried sheep. Anyway Lucky, it is time to get them moving again.'

Derek let Shep move forward again, and Shep closed in. Most of the sheep moved off as before, but a couple were quite happy where they were, doing a nice bit of grazing. Shep moved a bit closer. 'Was that a nip at their heels,' thought a surprised Derek. 'Surely not?'

In any event, the two mutineers leapt forward to join the others and forward progress was maintained until the next obstacle, in the shape of a large prickly hedge, was encountered. The sheep stopped and the dogs stopped. Shep didn't press on, unlike the slaughterhouse dogs, but instead he trotted up to the lead sheep.

The sheep spoke first.

'Look, we were quite happy to go along with this herding business, but now it's ended in this big prickly hedge. I don't see how, under the circumstances, we can continue.'[20]

Shep was nodding understandingly.

'Yes, considering the luscious un-grazed grass on the other side, this hedge must be a great disappointment to you. You say that under the circumstances you can't continue; would you therefore please help me by explaining those circumstances?'

Notes...

21.

If you see a solution to problems, don't be too eager to blurt it out. Build the problem to value the solution and then get commitment to move forward before solving the problem.

The sheep was relaxing, surprised by Shep's conciliatory attitude.

'We would all love fresh grazing but there is no apparent way through that prickly hedge, and you know what prickly hedges do to fleeces.'

Derek had seen a gap in the hedge and was so excited that he would be able to help. He started to rush forward to tell the sheep the good news.

'I can help with that!' he barked, 'There is a …'

Two things happened: the sheep's eyes opened with fear as it backed away, and Shep held up a restraining paw to stop Derek going any further.

'Excuse my young friend,' he said to the sheep. 'He is a little over-enthusiastic. Settle down Lucky – my colleague the sheep and I have a lot to discuss.'

A surprised Derek retreated and sat back down. Shep continued talking to the sheep.

'Yes, I agree there is nothing worse than a matted fleece, but I am sure you would agree that if you could get to the new grass, snag free, that would be marvellous?'

'Of course,' said the sheep. 'But I don't see a clear way through.'

Derek could hardly contain himself and thought he would explode, but Shep's paw rose again.[21]

'I can understand that. Look, if you could find a snag-free way through, would you go to the other side?'

'Of course,' said the sheep.

'Well,' said Shep, turning to the gap that Derek had seen, 'this leads comfortably through to the other side.'

'It's very narrow,' said the sheep.

Derek wanted to say, 'no it isn't,' but Shep's look stopped him.

'I'm so sorry to appear thick, but how do you mean, narrow?'

'Well, if we go through as a herd, the outside sheep will get snagged so it is too narrow.'

'I agree it is a little confined for a herd but if you would travel single file, there would be plenty of room. How could we help you to feel comfortable with that?'

'Perhaps if you went through first to prove it was safe and stayed away from us whilst we did it, I suppose it would be alright,' replied the sheep.

'OK,' said Shep, 'let's just run through that once again – to get things clear in my mind. You liked the idea of better grazing in the next field, you felt happy about us finding a way through and, if we kept a safe distance, you are happy to travel in single file? Yes?'

'Yes,' said the sheep.

'Well, I suggest we get things started by sending Lucky through. Go on Lucky, through you go and wait on the other side.'

Derek did as he was told and trotted through the gap in the hedge. He sat and waited, and it wasn't long before all the sheep came through in a long line.

At each obstacle, a similar process was repeated until they arrived at the pen. The problem was that the gate was shut.

'What now?' thought Derek as Shep picked up speed on the finishing stretch. Visions of colliding gates and sheep filled Derek's mind. Chaos would reign. But, smoothly and in good time, the shepherd stepped forward and held the gate open. He did it in such a way that the sheep were funnelled into the pen. They milled about bleating and jostling, but not in a panic, and Derek was surprised to hear their comments.

'Baa, best grass I've ever tasted.'

'Let me have some, baa.'

'Bleat, it feels jolly safe in here.'

Shep prowled round the perimeter, talking to the sheep.

Notes...

22.

Even when your customer has agreed to do business with you, you should praise and congratulate them. It makes them feel good and wish to repeat the experience over and over again.

'You've picked a good tuft here, probably the best in the field,' and 'I'm glad you're happy – can we do anything else for you?'[22]

As they trotted back to the farmyard, Derek was full of questions.

'The shepherd was nowhere to be seen, and then at the last moment he was there,' said Derek.

'That's the sign of a good boss – hands off, but always there to open gates when needed,' said Shep.

'And those sheep, they seemed really happy to be penned up,' Derek continued.

'Of course, I can do my job with confidence knowing that we are taking the sheep to a place in which they will be happy.'

'So then, it is important to do anything we can to make the sheep happy?' Derek felt that he was getting the idea.

Shep was thoughtful, 'Well sort of, but remember this is my job, my profession – I am a professional mover of sheep. I have pride in my success; I enjoy my high status as a reflection of my abilities and values. Of course, I do everything possible to make the sheep's life happy. I want them to be delighted with their destination and, probably more importantly, they must feel that they were treated excellently whilst they were being herded. I like to think of it as a journey but, and it is a big but, they will be herded because that is my job.'

'I can't get my head round this firm but nice thing,' said a getting-confused-again Derek. Before Shep could reply, they rounded a corner in the lane to see that the shepherd had stopped to chat to an old rosy-cheeked farmer who was leaning on a gate, just enjoying the sunshine and passing the time of day. At his side was a large pig, wearing the silly smile that pigs have when they are contented. The pig kept nudging and pushing its snout in and around the farmer's huge pocket in his hairy old tweed jacket.

'What you doin' girl?' the farmer enquired, scratching the pig's head. 'Do you think I've got an apple in there?'

The pig joyfully pushed its head against the farmer's hand as if to indicate that that is exactly what it thought.

This time the farmer tickled the pig's ear as he searched his own pocket.

'I can't fool you,' he said, producing a huge red apple, which he duly gave to the pig, who squealed and grunted with delight, whilst she made very short but messy work of the juicy fruit. With his hand still rubbing the pig's ear, the farmer turned back to the shepherd.

'This is Rosie,' he said, indicating the pig. 'She's a real beauty, aren't you girl?'

The pig replied with a grunt as it enjoyed the last morsels of apple.

'Yep, she's a good 'un,' he continued. 'She's going off to be bacon next week, aren't you girl.'

'*Bacon*?' Derek gasped to Shep. 'Bacon – you mean he is going to kill it?'

'I suppose so, unless you can think of a better way of making bacon,' sighed Shep, 'Tough old life.'

'I can't believe you can support that. How can he be so nice one minute and then talk about bacon the next.'

'I think that makes my point,' said Shep. 'Of course, you must be nice when you can but that guy is a pig farmer. He makes his living and feeds his family because he raises pigs for money. He doesn't have pet pigs.'

'OK,' said Derek, 'but why be so nice to the pig to then just go and kill it?'

'You stayed at Cold Valley Farm, didn't you?' asked Shep.

'Yes, but don't mention that place,' replied Derek, with a shudder.

'They kept pigs, didn't they?' continued Shep. 'What were their conditions like?'

Notes...

23.

Being good to the people we make our money out of should not cause a conflict. Nor should making money out of the people to whom we are good.

'Horrible,' remembered Derek. 'They were crammed together in huge dark sheds, packed so tightly that if one got ill or died, there wasn't enough room to fall over. Do you know, they used to get so frightened and frustrated that they would bite each others' tails off?'

'And then they would be bacon?' Shep asked wryly.

'Er, yes.'

'So, a life of pure misery and then bacon. You think that's better?'

'Er, no,' conceded Derek.

'Look, the point is, there should be no conflict between good treatment and making a living. On one hand, bad treatment does not produce a good return, but behaving well and living by the rules of care and consideration should not cause us to forget our own objectives.'[23]

As they walked on, Derek could see Shep's point of view but he resolved that, should he ever regain his human form, he would never eat bacon again. When they returned to the yard, Shep turned to Derek and said, 'I would get plenty of rest tonight, Lucky, because tomorrow you will be taking a whole herd from beginning to end, on your own. I think you are just about ready.'

That night, Derek tossed and turned, worrying about letting Shep down or making a fool of himself. When dawn came, he felt a bit ragged but determined to do his best. After a hearty breakfast and a pep talk from Shep, Derek was ready and they set off up to the fields. The shepherd patted Derek's head.

'There now Lucky, I see you're ready to go on your own. Good luck boy, off you go.'

They were on the knoll and Derek could see the sheep. He was eager to get started. He went to dart forward but Shep held up a paw.

'Whoa there, not so fast! What's the first thing?'

'Um.'

'No, not um, position. Where are the sheep?'

'Oh,' said a relieved Derek, 'there they are – I can see them,' and he went to leap forward again.

'No, hang on. I know you can see them but what is their exact position in relation to the whole job. How far are they away from the pen? What's their attitude towards being herded, and how many obstacles are there?'

Derek focused back; he could see the small group of sheep. In the distance he could see the pen and, in between, he saw a hedge, some trees, a gate, and a stream. He immediately panicked.

'Oh no, what a huge job, so many obstacles, so many sheep, such a small pen – can't I have an easier one?' he begged.

'Typical human attitude,' sighed Shep, but with a flicker of an understanding smile. 'Of course, to be a success we must have a clear overview of the whole task but, once we start, we dogs forget the obstacles behind, and the obstacles to come, and we deal with the ones of the moment. Remember that prickly hedge – remember the farting cat – we solved that one by concentrating one hundred per cent and not being distracted by worry. How would you eat an elephant?'

'A what?'

'An elephant. I'll tell you. You would eat it one piece at a time. Off you go now, one piece at a time.'[24]

Off Derek set, nervous but determined. He moved in on the sheep just as he had been taught and they moved off. It was all a bit ragged but they were moving, and moving well. His heart was in his mouth as they came to the stream, which was the first obstacle, but the sheep, although concerned about the water, seemed quite happy to work with Derek and they crossed it together. It was tough but it was going well. A bit too well actually, so much so that Derek

Notes...

24.

If you run a small business, the obstacles between you and those valuable customers are daunting. But seeing them is half the battle; knocking them down one at a time is the other half. And no, you can't have easier targets!

suspected that Shep had had a paw in selecting this group of sheep and probably had had a word with them into the bargain. Perhaps he was getting over confident, or he was letting his mind wander, but, inadvertently, Derek had upped the pace to a point where the sheep were on the edge of being beyond control. He spotted his mistake too late as he realized the sheep were running ahead, somewhat out of his influence and, to his horror, ahead he could see an open gate.

'The beet field!'

His heart sank, 'Once those sheep get into that crop, good sheep or not, all will be lost.'

The sheep were way ahead of Derek as he prepared to accept his fate but, as they approached the gate, a large fierce dog blocked their way. It was Butch – miserable, old, not-Derek's-friend, Butch – who was there to save the day. The sheep slackened their pace and turned. The old dog gave Derek a huge wink and barked out, 'You're doing a good job, Lucky, keep it up lad!'

Praise indeed. Derek felt like a million dollars and soon he was clearing the other obstacles one after another. Now for the big one: the pen lay ahead and the sheep could feel Derek's excitement and anxiety. They were becoming frisky and ragged.

Notes...

25.

They used to call it closing the sale; we could call it proposing action, but whatever. The big tragedy is doing all that great work of obstacle removing and herding, to lose it all in sight of victory — without getting that vital action.

'Maybe this is enough for one session,' thought Derek and he started to back off, and stop.

'The job's not done until it's done,' called Shep. 'Don't waste all that great effort now. Finish the job and put them in the pen.'

One last effort, the shepherd opened the gate. The sheep were worrying and starting to break apart, but the shepherd reached as far as he could with his crook to make the opening huge and Derek, somewhat out of control, got the sheep in the pen. The gate slammed shut and the other dogs let out a huge cheer. Derek felt fantastic.[25]

'Success at last,' he thought, but he was a little surprised that there was no sign of the witch's spell breaking. Perhaps it wears off slowly. As they trotted back to the farm, Derek mentioned Butch.

'It was Butch that saved me there,' said Derek. 'I thought he hated me.'[26]

'There are two things that happened there,' replied Shep. 'One is that Butch is a team player, he wants the group to succeed, and he sees his pride and status tied up with all of us. His loyalty, ability and effort are things he brings to work. When he isn't working, he can be different. You humans can never separate personality from the problem, so you bring all sorts of mental baggage to work which just about

Notes...

26.

You don't have to be pals outside work to pull together as a great team. Separate people from the problem.

guarantees failure. Sit on that grassy knoll, get a clear view, and get the job done. Butch saw the job to be done and did it. Personality had nothing to do with it.'

'And second?' asked Derek.

'Second? Oh, yes. And second, your behaviour is winning respect from all of us and, do you know, I think Butch is starting to like you.'

Over the next days, the witch's spell didn't seem to be wearing off but, in a way, Derek didn't mind all that much. He threw himself into the work. Sometimes he made huge mistakes but, although not perfect, he felt that he was making progress. Then one day, he woke up and the whole farmyard was buzzing with excitement. Even Shep's usual equanimity seemed a little ruffled.

'What's going on?' asked Derek.

'It's the big one,' a dog replied. 'The sheepdog trials grand prix is on in a week's time. The dogs that win that competition will be acknowledged as the best in the world.'

'I'd like to see that,' exclaimed Derek.

'Like to see it? You'll be in it, Lucky.'

Derek spun round to look at Shep, who continued, 'It's a team effort. Every one of us will have something to do and that includes you. Don't worry, we are good. It is really a two-horse race: us, or Cold Valley Farm. And I'm sure you would like a chance to show them up.'

Derek wasn't sure. Cold Valley was a horrible place, but there was little doubting their cold professionalism and their ruthless quest for success. Nonetheless, Derek threw himself in with the rest, practising for the big day, fairly content in the knowledge that his fellow dogs were brilliant, and that he was only to play a minor role.

The great day came, and the dogs were trucked in and unloaded at the enormous show ground. Derek saw the awful owner of Cold Valley Farm arguing with their shepherd. He was pointing at Derek and Fido, obviously trying to claim ownership of what were now clearly very fit dogs. The shepherd would have none of it and pointed out that they were both strays that had run away when shot at. The man saw that he hadn't much chance of pressing his case, but it was clear that the whole contest would be overshadowed by considerable ill feeling.

In the waiting ring, Shep, Derek, and Fido were together but, just feet away, stood Patch, Brutus, and Dodger. Brutus bared his teeth at Derek and snarled, 'I should have torn your throat out when I had the chance.' He took a step forward. Shep casually stepped in to put himself between Brutus and Derek.

'I'm sorry Brutus, I didn't quite catch that. Is there anything I can help you with?'

The two dogs' eyes locked and, after some time, it was Brutus who broke away.

'Dead meat, you are, dead meat,' he called to Derek over his shoulder.

The contest was close. The Cold Valley Farm dogs were cold, pushy and efficient, but their aggression didn't exactly win them friends amongst the sheep. Derek's team were full of enthusiasm and worked well with the sheep, but occasionally their inexperience showed. Finally the result was announced. It was an unprecedented dead heat – there would have to be a tiebreak. Two dogs' names would be picked at random from a hat and they would have a new flock of sheep each, with one ram – also picked at random.

There was an agonizing wait and then the loud-speaker crackled into life.

'The dog representing Cold Valley Farm will be …,' there was the sound of rustling paper, 'Brutus!'

If dogs could punch the air with their paws, the Cold Valley pack would have done so.

'And, for Sunnydale …,' more rustling as the tension became unbearable, 'Lucky!'

Derek's heart sank.

'I'm so sorry, Shep,' he gasped, 'it wasn't my fault.'

Shep looked at him with a firm look.

'Listen, we can't hide the fact that the odds are stacked against you, but you are one of our team and we know you will do your best. We couldn't ask for more, win or lose won't change the way we feel. At least Brutus is going first so you can watch him and try to see the best way. You are called Lucky, so think Lucky.'

Despite Shep's encouraging words, Derek felt awful. All he could do was remember what he had learned and try to stay in control.

His reverie was shattered as the Cold Valley farmer called his dog with a piercing whistle. Derek could see the group of sheep and tried to position them in relation to the rest of the course. Brutus was clearly in no need of such thought and shot forward like greased lightning. Soon the sheep were moving, and Brutus' performance could only be described as cool, confident, fast, and efficient. He even had time to flash the odd sneering snarl in Derek's direction and mouth 'dead meat' at him.

Derek felt horribly intimidated but tried to watch the whole run. As well as obstacles, there were numbered marker posts, which the herd had to round.

'If I go by the numbers, at least I'll know where I am and how well I'm doing,' thought Derek.

Brutus cleared each obstacle and marker faultlessly, and it was impossible to see where he had dropped even one point. Soon he was in the finishing straight and, as they neared the pen, the farmer opened the gate. However, he did it a bit suddenly and the front sheep dodged slightly. Because of Brutus' confidence – probably arrogance – he had taken the speed of the sheep to the very edge of control. A lesser dog could not possibly have taken sheep at that speed but, when that sheep moved, it took the whole flock beyond his influence. A large ewe broke away and Brutus, realizing his mistake, struck like a snake to regain control, which he would have done had his farmer not panicked. He thought Brutus had blown it and, in a rage, lifted his crook as if to strike the dog.

'Grrrrh, you stupid dog!'

Brutus instinctively ducked and, in the process, let a ewe slip by. However, the loss of control was short lived and the sheep were soon contained, and herded

Notes...

27.

Everybody likes to be asked for help. If you are young and inexperienced, don't ever pretend that you aren't. The tough, old, hard-bitten veteran, more often than not, will come to your side if you respect their ability to help and advise. Don't be afraid to ask.

in an orderly fashion into the pen. One mistake, but on the whole a brilliant performance.

'Brutus scores ninety-five!'

Less than five points dropped: a stunning performance. Derek felt anxious beyond belief when, as if in a dream, he heard his shepherd's whistle. Shep was at his side, 'Go on Lucky, good luck!'

Derek trotted forward as his group of sheep were herded into the arena. Just when he thought things couldn't get any worse, to his horror he saw leading the flock none other than the dreaded Reg the ram.

'Go on,' called the shepherd, and Derek set off feeling distinctly less than cheery.

'Oh well,' he thought. 'I suppose I can't make it any worse if I try to remember what I have learned. First, a clear overview; where are the sheep now; how big is the distance; how many obstacles are there; do I clearly see and understand where the pen is?' He moved forward to battle with Reg. 'Coming away alive would be a result,' thought Derek gloomily.[27]

As he closed in on the sheep, the huge battle-scarred ram lowered its head ready to charge. The dogs from Cold Valley sniggered in glee at the sight of not only victory in their grasp but also an old enemy battered to death. The normally placid Shep snarled at them and they shut up – but nothing could disguise their joy.

Derek wanted to run away but instead he spoke to Reg.

'Um, hello.'

'Hello yourself,' snapped back Reg, 'I remember you. Last time we met I half killed you. Do you want me to finish the job or have you learned your lesson?'

'I certainly have learned my lesson, but I am in a real bind. I wonder if you could help me?' Derek stood quietly waiting for the impact, but instead ...

'Help you! Why on earth would I help you?'

'No reason particularly, but may I ask you something?'

Derek waited, and waited some more.

'Go on, but don't waste my time.'

'I am a very inexperienced sheepdog, I make loads of mistakes but we really do have a wonderful pen full of lush grass for the sheep. You are the most experienced and senior sheep I know. If you were in my position, how would you go about the herding?'

Reg looked at him long and hard to see if he could detect even a flicker of insincerity.

'I've been at this game a long time,' stated Reg.

'I know,' said Derek. 'That's why your advice would be so helpful.'

'I eat dogs like you for breakfast.'

'I know, that's why I would like you to tell me how you should be treated. I would be so excited if I could work with you. So where do I start?'

'First lad, don't come charging up to me expecting to intimidate. Bigger boys than you have tried and failed.'

Derek remembered the German shepherds and shuddered.

'No, give me some space and I'll move in my own time, and when I move, the other sheep move with me, like this.'

With that, Reg started trotting off and the other sheep went with him, just like he said.

The watching dogs were stunned.

'He got them moving!' said Dodger to Patch, and got a very nasty bite for his trouble.

Derek trotted alongside Reg. 'Was this some sort of sly trickery?' he wondered, 'No!' He realized he was growing to like and respect the old ram now that he was starting to get to know him. He even began to chat as they trundled along.

'Gosh, you terrified me when we first met,' observed Derek.

'Don't like being pushed,' replied Reg.

Notes...

28.

Watch out for markers and landmarks on your journey; they show you that you are herding in the right direction.

Rule: always know where you are, how much you have done, and how much you need to do.

Derek looked up to see the approaching marker – *two*! A great big number two! They hadn't passed one; the sheep were going in the wrong direction.

Derek started to panic, perhaps he should bark a warning or run in front of the sheep to stop them but, before he could do anything, Reg noticed Derek's distress and saw the situation.[28]

'Nay, lad, don't do anything hasty. The flock's just following the contours of the land. You've got a nice steady pace going, now just move alongside gently on the opposite side to where you want them to go. That way they'll think they are still choosing their own direction.'

'Thanks Reg,' Derek panted, and he followed the ram's instructions to the letter. And, sure enough, the flock started to gently turn towards the number '1' marker, but Derek had left it a bit late and they were all heading straight for the post, not round it. The danger was that it could split them, and then all would be lost. Derek was scared of upsetting the sheep but he decided to get closer and, as he did so, the turn increased and, with a gasp from the crowd, they cleared number one by barely an inch.

'That lost me a few points,' thought Derek gloomily.

Notes...

29.

A real favourite: even when all is lost and you are being carried to the car park by security, look over your shoulder and cry, 'I would love to do business with you, please tell me what I need to do'. You will often be told, and then it is up to you what happens next.

The next post went better because Derek was planning well ahead. This steady progress was interrupted by their arrival at the stream, where the sheep just stopped.

'How had Brutus done it?' wondered Derek. He realized that Brutus had just kept up his blistering pace and the sheep were more frightened of Brutus than the water. The problem was that nobody was frightened of Derek.

'What now?'

'Work with us, lad,' Reg interrupted Derek's ruminations, 'The flock likes you and is starting to trust you.'

'So why are they objecting to crossing the stream?' asked Derek.

'They are not objecting – they have concerns about the stream. Be their friend; help them with their concerns.'

'I don't know what their concerns are,' said Derek.

'Then ask them,' suggested Reg.

Derek turned to a large ewe, 'We were going along so nicely, what have I got to do to help you cross this stream?'[29]

'Baa, we're worried that the water is too deep. Sheep can't swim very well, you know.'

Notes...

30.

Another classic for dealing with concerns: instead of answering the question, 'No, it's too dear,' with 'No it isn't,' try this:

'No, it's too dear.'
'I can understand your concerns but, to clear things up in my mind, what exactly do you mean, <u>too dear?</u>'

When they explain, you will have a solution.

'I understand exactly what you are saying but *deep*, how do you mean deep?'[30]

'Well, if it comes over our knees then we are in trouble.'

The other dogs and the crowd wondered what was going on as the flock and Derek stood with the clock ticking away, but Derek continued, it was his only chance.

'Is that your only concern?'

'Baa, yes it is.'

'Ok then, if I can show you that the water is shallow enough, will you cross?'

'Yes we will,' the sheep bleated together.

The crowd were astonished to see Derek turn away from the flock and trot across the stream on his own.

'Has he given up?' wondered Fido.

'Well, you can't herd from the front,' sneered Patch.

'Just watch,' said Shep calmly.

There were cries of amazement when a few moments later the whole flock crossed and were soon moving at a good pace again.

Obstacle after obstacle was cleared, it wasn't the tidiest or the fastest performance but steady, measurable progress was made. Derek stayed calm

Notes...

31.

During the journey, write down all things the other party liked. When the end is in sight, list all the things that they liked, get them to agree that they liked those things, and then propose the action.

and remembered to think like a dog. He didn't dwell on past mistakes and, although he had a clear plan of the whole route in his mind, he dealt with each obstacle as he came to it, giving each one a hundred per cent of his attention instead of stressing about future problems.

Soon, it was their turn for the finishing straight. Derek started to worry. He and the sheep had worked well together; they had cleared obstacles together and had worked with each other's concerns. Would he risk that great relationship by pushing them one step too far, by driving them into the pen. Then he remembered the pig and the other lessons he had learned. This was his job, the culmination of all the effort. The pen was the goal – without the finish there was no point.[31]

'OK, sheep,' he called, 'may I ask you something?'

The sheep stopped to listen.

'OK, you agreed that your present grazing was wearing a little bit thin.'

'Baa, yes.'

'You felt that a nice trot in the fresh grass would be nice?'

'Baa, yes.'

'You agreed that lush green grass would make your fleece, well, er, fleecier?'

'Baa, yes.'

'And you agreed that the best grass was there in that pen?'

'Baa, yes.'

'OK, may I suggest this? When the shepherd opens the gate to the pen, you all go inside and start enjoying that super grass?'

'Baa, yes.'

The shepherd opened the gate and everyone's jaw dropped as Derek sat without moving a muscle and the sheep ambled happily into the pen where they grazed contentedly.

'Reg,' Derek called.

The ram turned.

'Thank you so much – I couldn't have done it without you.'

The ram replied, 'Well, I never thought I'd like a dog, but for you I will make an exception.'

Derek joined the other dogs and they waited for the result. The speakers crackled into life.

'We now have the final score. Cold Valley Farm with Brutus has scored ninety-five. Sunnydale Farm with Lucky has scored ninety-five ...,'

'Oh, a tie again,' thought Derek, but the speaker crackled again.

'… point five.'

'Ninety-five point five!' Derek's heart leapt. 'We've won, we beat them by half a point.'

Shep and the others went wild barking with joy.

'Lucky did it for us! Lucky is our hero!'

Derek had never felt happier but, on the other hand, never more peculiar.

'I don't feel well,' he gasped, and ran behind some caravans. There was a flash and a smell of old fireworks. He was on all fours, but his fur had gone, his paws were now hands and feet. As he pulled himself upright, he realized he was a man again.

'Happy now?' came a voice from behind him. It was Shep.

'I can still understand you, my friend,' gasped Derek.

'Once a dog, always a dog – on the inside anyway. You will always know the way of the dog,' said Shep. 'Now I bet your family would like to see you again. By the way, I'm not sure it is acceptable for humans to appear like that.'

Derek realized he was stark naked and blowing in the wind was that day's financial pages, which he quickly fashioned into a loincloth.

'Well, can't sit here all day,' said Shep. 'Got a victory to celebrate. Go home Lucky, but don't forget us.'

'I won't,' said Derek feeling choked, but happy to be going home.

As he headed back he adjusted his newspaper to its most decorous position and an advert caught his eye. 'Major multi-national seeks sales director'.

As Derek jogged along the street, appearing for all the world like a sort of city-based Tarzan, a king of the urban jungle, he felt such energy. He believed that he could do anything as people turned and stared at this man of bronze. A huge skyscraper caught his eye, and the name in lights on the top rang a bell: it was the company in the job advert. Perhaps he would think about getting an application form. Perhaps he should think it over. Perhaps he didn't have enough experience. Perhaps this wasn't the best time. Perhaps the receptionist would not let him speak to the right people. Perhaps he wasn't dressed correctly. That was the last tiny vestige of the old Derek speaking. Perhaps he would go for it right now!

The Board were stunned when the entrance of a fit, tanned man, with a pierced ear and wearing nothing but the financial pages, interrupted their meeting.

'I saw your ad,' said the apparition, pointing strategically to his strange attire, 'and I am the one you are looking for.'

There was no doubt. Everyone in the room knew he was right. All they could say was, 'When can you start?'

'I haven't actually seen my family for a while, and I had better get a more appropriate outfit. What about next week, or would the week after be better for you?'

The Board's mouths moved like goldfish. All they could say was 'Whenever you like.'

'Next week, then,' Derek smiled and started to leave.

The Chief Executive finally regained the power of speech, 'I'm sorry, we didn't get your name.'

'Oh, my name? My name is Derek Stubbins, but my friends all call me Lucky!'[32]

Notes...

32. Shepherd's thoughts

When the story started, our hero was a pretty dire employee. The shepherd's careful management and the use of his best team members created success from failure. Could you do that for someone who worked for you?

The Way of the Dog

In a Nutshell

Start

Position

Asking questions is the best way to find both their position and your position. Don't even think of starting the journey until you know the position.

- *Tip* – talk about the past
- *Try* – who did this for you, when did you decide, how is this done, and what were you spending?

The lift

The only time the pressure should be raised is when we start them moving. Change is usually resisted. Take and keep control. Propose action, give no choice. CHOICES: 'tomorrow, or the day after?'

The obstacles

Find all the obstacles and remove them. The only thing that is between you and success are obstacles. Therefore, when the obstacles are removed, success is inevitable. Become their partner, see the obstacles as their concerns, work together to reassure and remove these concerns.

The pen

Get someone in a position of power to help open gates for you. Realize that you have done all that work and don't waste it by giving up at the gate of the pen. They may be very interested, but you will have to guide them in.

Looking after your flock

The journey could be one interaction or a lifetime's relationship. Keep them happy by congratulating them on their choices. Don't let others damage what you have worked for.

About the Author

Geoff Burch

Geoff Burch is often to be found trundling around the world giving his powerful, and hopefully funny, motivational presentations. If enough pressure is applied, he can even be persuaded to perform 'The Way of the Dog', complete with barking, scampering, and bleating!

Geoff can be contacted through his website, **www.geoffburch.com**.